Thermodynamic Cycles

Effective Modeling Strategies
for Software Development

by D. James Benton

Preface

Efficient design, operation, and maintenance of power and process systems require accurate and effective thermodynamic cycle modeling tools. Many such tools exist; however, the logic and programming of these tools vary considerably, making them more or less practical for differing applications. This book is a compilation of what to do and what to avoid, including the details of how to best accomplish the desired end. All of the data and source code are available free online.

All of the examples contained in this book,
(as well as a lot of free programs) are available at...

https://www.dudleybenton.altervista.org/software/index.html

Programming

All of the examples presented in this book are implemented either in the C programming language or Excel® macros. The code, spreadsheets, data files, and other material are arranged in folders within a single ZIP archive that can be freely downloaded at the address above. A conventional cycle modeling tool (QUEST described in Appendix C) is freely available at this time. It currently has only rudimentary interactive features, but will eventually be fully-developed. A more general thermodynamic cycle modeling tool (CyclePro) is currently under development and will eventually become open source. CyclePro can already import models from GateCycle® and PEPSE®.

Additional Material

Additional material on thermodynamics can be found at:

https://www.amazon.com/dp/B01M31ZP8R

More on heat exchangers can be found at:

https://www.amazon.com/dp/B078HM16GV

Property formulations, code, and Excel Add-Ins can be found at:

https://www.amazon.com/dp/B07Q5L1CHT

Moist air properties, formulations, code, and Excel Add-Ins can be found at:

https://www.amazon.com/dp/B06XSRW4DK

As this material is readily available, these topics will only be covered briefly in this text.

Copyright/Trademark Notices

Excel® is a product of Microsoft®. GateCycle™ is a trademark of the General Electric Company. PEPSE® is marketed by Curtiss-Wright.

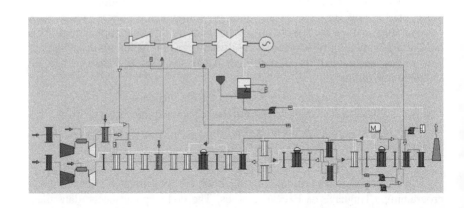

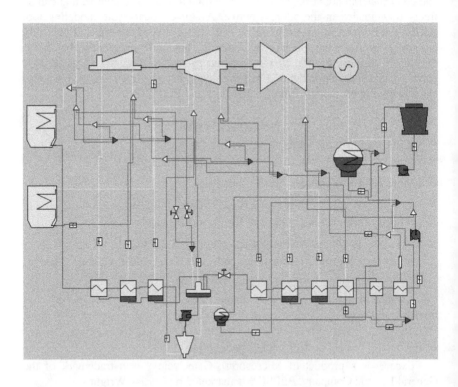

Table of Contents   page

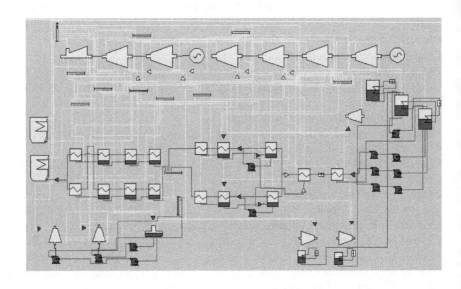

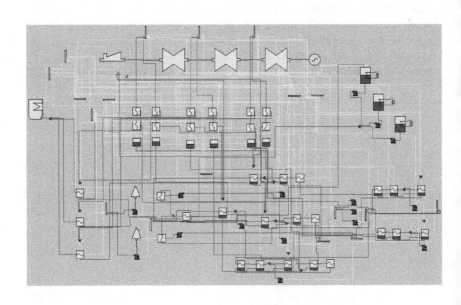

Chapter 1. Introduction

Thermodynamic cycle modeling can be divided into three parts: 1) properties, 2) components, and 3) ensemble. The whole will be not better than the weakest part. This chapter provides an overview of these three parts and the following chapters provide the details. After that, we will work through several complete examples for different types of systems.

Properties

Properties are divided into three categories: 1) thermodynamic, 2) physical, and 3) chemical. The first group includes: pressure, temperature, specific volume (or density), enthalpy (or specific heat), and entropy. The second group includes: viscosity, thermal conductivity, surface tension, and diffusivity. The third group includes: molecular weight, heat (and entropy) of formation, and heat (and entropy) of combustion.

Thermodynamic properties must always be formulated in terms of temperature and density (or specific volume). Pressure and temperature are not independent and formulations based on these (e.g., ASME-67[1] and IAPWS-IF97[2]) are just a mess. Avoid them. For steam you will want to use: KKHM-69[3], NBS/NRC-84[4], or IAPWS-SF95.[5] You will need steam properties for several of the spreadsheets described herein. You are welcome to use the following free Excel® Add-In for academic (non-commercial) purposes. All of the source files can be found in the examples\AllSteam folder of the freely available online archive for this text.

https://dudleybenton.altervista.org/miscellaneous/AllSteam103.zip

The only properties of moist air considered are those developed by Hyland & Wexler[6,7,8], and refined by Nelson & Sauer.[9] The more recent formulation

---

[1] Meyer, C. A., McClintock, R. B., Silvestri, G. J., and Spencer, R. C., Jr., *Thermodynamic and Transport Properties of Steam*, American Society of Mechanical Engineers, 1967.

[2] Research and Technology Committee on Water and Steam in Thermal Power Systems, *ASME Steam Properties for Industrial Use*, The American Society of Mechanical Engineers, 1997.

[3] Keenan, J. H., Keyes, F. G., Hill, P. G., and Moore, J. G., *Steam Tables*, John Wiley & Sons, Inc., 1969.

[4] Haar, L., Gallagher, J. S., and Kell, G. S., *Steam Tables*, NBS/NRC printed by Hemisphere, distributed by McGraw-Hill, 1984.

[5] Friend, D. G. and Dooley, R. B., *Revised Formulation for the Thermodynamic Properties of Ordinary Water Substance for General and Scientific Use*, The International Association for the Properties of Water and Steam, 1995.

[6] Hyland, R. W., Wexler, A., and Stewart, R., "Thermodynamic Properties of Dry Air, Moist Air and Water and SI Psychrometric Charts," ASHRAE RP-216 and RP-25, 1983.

developed by Hermann, Kretzschmar, and Gatley[1011]do not constitute a substantive improvement, merely an academic one. There is no point implementing these. You will need moist air properties for several of the spreadsheets described herein. You are welcome to use the following free Excel® Add-In:

https://dudleybenton.altervista.org/software/Psychrometrics_V100.ZIP

Moist air properties appear in various editions of the *ASHRAE Handbook of Fundamentals*. Beware that the equations in many editions of this otherwise excellent reference are wrong in that the equations contained therein don't produce the tabulated results. In 1984 this author was part of a Cooling Technology Institute (CTI) task force investigating discrepancies in the published properties of moist air. The National Bureau of Standards (now National Institute of Standards and Technology) lost Hyland & Wexler's original reports; however, a copy still existed in the Library of Congress (LOC). A colleague, Al Feltzin, went to the LOC and made a photocopy of the original reports. The tabulated values in the ASHRAE handbook are correct, but not all of the equations are, especially before 1993. Formulations consistent with Hyland & Wexler, along with code plus an Excel® Add-In can be found in my book , *Evaporative Cooling*, and on my web site listed in the foreword.

Chemical properties are most often simply tabulated. The two most common references are the *CRC Handbook of Chemistry and Physics* (numerous editions published by CRC Press) and *Lange's Handbook of Chemistry* (McGraw-Hill). The Engineering Toolbox is a good online source:

https://www.engineeringtoolbox.com/

Components

Each type of component must be modeled differently. The major types will be handled in subsequent separate chapters. The accuracy of the whole depends on each of the components. In all cases, components are seen as acting on

---

[7] Hyland, R. W. and Wexler, A., "Formulations for the Thermodynamic Properties of the Saturated Phases of H2O from 173.15 K to 473.15 K," ASHRAE Trans., Vol. 89, pp. 500-519, 1983.

[8] Hyland, R. W. and Wexler, A., "Formulations for the Thermodynamic Properties of Dry Air from 173.15 K to 473.15 K, and of Saturated Moist Air from 173.15 K to 372.15 K, at Pressures to 5 MPa," ASHRAE Trans., Vol. 89, pp. 520-535, 1983.

[9] Nelson, H. F. and Sauer, H. J., "Formulation of High-Temperature Properties for Moist Air," HVAC&R Research Vol. 8, pp. 311-334, 2002.

[10] Herrmann, S., Kretzschmar, H.-J., and Gatley, D. P., "Thermodynamic Properties of Real Moist Air, Dry Air, Steam, Water, and Ice," HVAC&R Research, 2009.

[11] Herrmann, S., Kretzschmar, H.-J., and Gatley, D. P., "Thermodynamic Properties of Real Moist Air, Dry Air, Steam, Water, and Ice - Final Report," ASHRAE RP-1485, 2009.

various streams. That is, something goes in and is different when it comes out. We do not consider the reverse, that is, something comes out; therefore, something different must have gone in. This reverse process is ambiguous at best and computationally problematic. While some commercial thermodynamic cycle models do solve system in this way, it is not robust to do so and only adds unnecessary additional work for the engineer.

Ensemble

How to put it all together? First of all, temperature is not conserved, so it's not going to be a primary variable. Mass, force, and energy are conserved. These are the *only* primary variables. We will work with mass (not volumetric) flow, pressure, and enthalpy. These quantities propagate (or transfer) in *only* one direction: downstream. Information does not naturally flow upstream. If you develop a model presuming that it does, you are creating problems for yourself and any subsequent users.

There's no such thing as pressure (or any other type) of "signals" that magically propagate around a computational model and make things happen. While it is true that the swallowing capacity of the various stages of a steam turbine ultimately links the pressures in the evaporators to the flows, computer models don't work this way. If you try and force a computer model to work this way, you will regret it. If you want to establish a link between a flow and a pressure, that's what macros are for. What's the difference? The former is implicit and the latter is explicit.

When modeling thermodynamic cycles, the solution of each component should follow this path: $P2=P1+\Delta P$, $H2=H1+\Delta H$, $T2=TofPH(P2,H2)$. That is, you first balance force and energy, then calculate secondary properties, such as temperature. Conservation of mass follows in the same manner, for example: $M3=M1+M2$. It is most effective to conserve mass before force and energy, but this order is less critical than calculating temperature from enthalpy rather than the other way around. If your model follows any other path, you're not working with the primary (i.e., conserved) quantities. Following this order means that much (if not most) of the computational effort will be devoted to implicit property calls (e.g., TofPH rather than HofTP), which should be implemented as efficiently as possible.

Consistency

This is perhaps the most basic feature of any computer model. The steps laid out in the preceding section assure internal consistency. External consistency means at least getting the same answer twice, though is often more than that. Unless you're running a Monte Carlo model, it had better produce exactly the same final results when given the same inputs. Sadly, this is not true for what is otherwise one of the most remarkable tools ever developed: GateCycle™. Every time you run it, you get a different answer. This is because

3

the previous results are the starting point in an iterative process. This is unacceptable and should be unthinkable for a programmer. No amount of time savings is worth the price of this outcome.

If you run a GateCycle™ model at 0, 10, 20, 30, 40°C ambient, you will get different results than if you run it at 40, 30, 20, 10, 0°C ambient. Sometimes the results are more than slightly different. Should the model fail to converge, you may be faced with building the model all over again, as the messed-up results are written back into the input file and will be used to start the next run. For this reason, periodic back-ups are highly recommended when using GateCycle™. It is quite remarkable how rapidly GateCycle™ converges for some cases, but this is hardly worth the anxiety it costs.

Organization of the Text

The rest of this text is roughly divided into three sections. The first section covers components found in conventional power systems followed by examples of how these are solved. The second section covers components found in gas turbine combined cycle plants followed by examples of how these are solved. The third section covers unconventional cycles, components, and solution techniques.

4

Chapter 2. Steam Condensers

As the temperature on the condensing side of these heat exchangers is approximately uniform, there is no significant difference between the LMTD and NTU-effectiveness methods. You might calculate an average specific heat for the cold side of a water-cooled or air-cooled condenser, but this is rarely necessary for the conditions in which these operate. Property differences are miniscule compared to the other variables associated with these system components.

Water-Cooled Steam Surface Condensers

The two key references for water-cooled condensers are: ASME PTC-12.2 (2010) and the Heat Exchange Institute Standards for Steam Surface Condensers 11th Ed. (2012). These two documents are quite different in approach and content, the former is more academic and the latter is more practical. PTC-12.2 presents dimensionless correlations involving Reynolds and Nusselt numbers and the HEI document contains lots of interesting tables and curves.

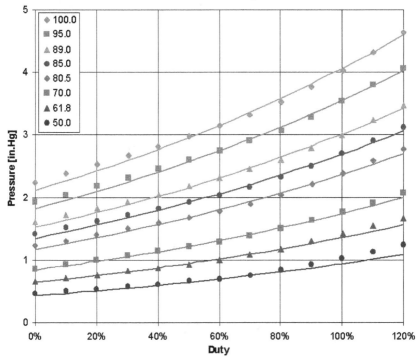

The primary concern of these documents and various formulas therein is to estimate a value for the overall heat transfer coefficient, U. Unless you happen to work for a condenser manufacturer, you will be supplied with this

5

information directly or indirectly. Most often the overall heat transfer coefficient will be supplied implicitly in the form of curves, such as the preceding figure.

The points in the preceding figure were digitized from the manufacturer's curves and the curves are a bivariate first-order regression. The design point is: 233,500 gpm water flow, 300,197 ft² surface area, and 2304 MBTU/hr.[12,13] Before we discuss the regression, we will consider the heat transfer, which is given by the following equation:

$$\dot{m}_{water}Cp_{water}\Delta T_{water} = \dot{m}_{steam}\Delta H_{steam} = UA \cdot LMTD \qquad (2.1)$$

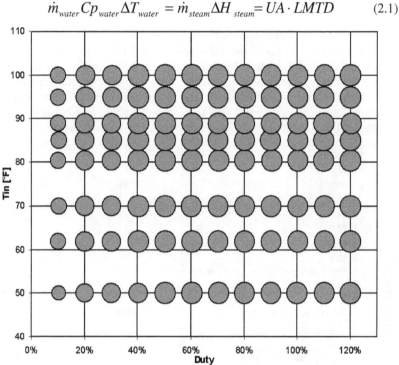

The digitized points, calculations, and figures can be found in the examples\ condensers folder in spreadsheet water_cooled_condenser.xls, an excerpt of which appears on the next page. A graph of UA appears on the preceding page.

	A	B	C	D	E	F	G	H
1	typical water-cooled steam surface condenser curves							
2	Tin	Duty	Pres.	Tsat	Q	Tout	LMTD	UA
3	°F	%	in.Hg	°F	MBTU/hr	°F	°F	MBTU/hr/°F
4	50.0	0%	0.46	56.0	0	50.0	0.0	
5	50.0	10%	0.50	58.6	237	52.0	4.5	52
6	50.0	20%	0.53	60.1	462	54.0	6.5	71
7	50.0	30%	0.58	62.4	694	55.9	8.8	79
8	50.0	40%	0.61	64.1	923	57.9	10.7	86
9	50.0	50%	0.66	66.2	1156	59.9	12.8	91
10	50.0	60%	0.70	67.7	1388	61.9	14.6	95
11	50.0	70%	0.75	69.9	1617	63.9	16.7	97
12	50.0	80%	0.83	73.0	1846	65.8	19.2	96
13	50.0	90%	0.92	76.1	2075	67.8	21.7	96
14	50.0	100%	1.02	79.2	2304	69.7	24.2	95
15	50.0	110%	1.12	82.1	2537	71.7	26.6	95
16	50.0	120%	1.24	85.2	2766	73.7	29.1	95
17	61.8	0%	0.65	65.6	0	61.8	0.0	
18	61.8	10%	0.70	67.9	233	63.8	3.7	63
19	61.8	20%	0.76	70.1	466	65.8	5.9	79
20	61.8	30%	0.82	72.5	695	67.7	8.1	86
21	61.8	40%	0.87	74.1	923	69.7	10.0	93
22	61.8	50%	0.93	76.3	1156	71.7	12.0	96
23	61.8	60%	0.99	78.3	1389	73.7	14.1	99
24	61.8	70%	1.09	81.0	1614	75.6	16.4	99
25	61.8	80%	1.18	83.5	1847	77.6	18.6	99
26	61.8	90%	1.30	86.5	2075	79.6	21.1	99
27	61.8	100%	1.41	89.3	2308	81.6	23.4	98
28	61.8	110%	1.54	92.1	2537	83.5	25.8	98
29	61.8	120%	1.66	94.6	2766	85.5	28.0	99

There is a consistent pattern, which can be seen in the smaller orange circles to the left side (low duty) and in each column of results (e.g., 52, 71, 79, ..., 95, 95, 95). This is not digitizing error, nor is it an artifact of generating and transmitting the graph. No condenser manufacturer wants to guarantee the performance (i.e., pressure or vacuum) at very low duty. No industrial condenser is without leaks, nor condensate without impurities and non-condensibles. Each manufacturer has their own "tweak" to adjust the pressures upward on the left side (low duty) of the performance curves. You may or may not want to include this in your calculations. If you do, you will need a higher order regression. Some manufacturers employ a "tweak" that results in a discontinuous slope of the curves on the left side, in which case a simple higher order regression will not produce a discontinuity. In that case, you will need to build in some sort of if()then else statement or utilize a two-dimensional table of values. GateCycle™ can handle either a macro or a 2D table.

If we plot the saturation temperature rather than the steam pressure, the lines flatten out and the bivariate first-order correlation becomes apparent.

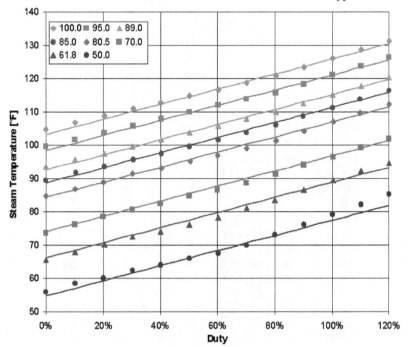

The bivariate first-order regression is shown in the first figure on the next page along with the R^2 and line of exact agreement. The regression is performed using the Excel® LINEST function in cells AC3:AE8. The regression coefficient (R^2) is in cell AC5 and the total residual is in cell AD8. You can select which steam properties to use (i.e., 67, 69, 84, 95, or 97) by changing cell J1. All of these details can be found on the first tab, Sheet1.

We will now consider two ways to implement this component in a thermodynamic cycle model. The first is illustrated on the second tab, Sheet2, as shown in the second figure on the next page. The adjustable parameters (i.e., user inputs) are in the top section and the calculations are in the bottom section. The saturation temperature (or pressure) is adjusted until the UA matches some target, in this case the average, which is in cell AA6 on the first tab.

8

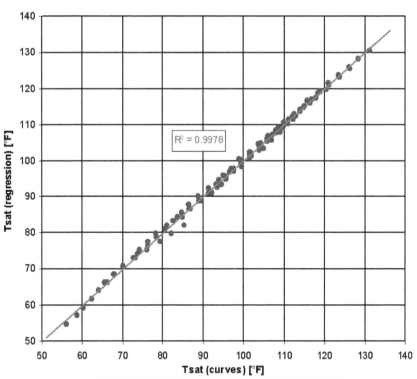

	A	B	C
1	**Operating Point**		
2	User Inputs		
3	water inlet temperature	67.3	°F
4	cooling water flow	200,000	gpm
5	steam flow	2,500,000	lbm/hr
6	steam quality	89.5%	
7	Calculations		
8	saturation temperature	99.8	°F
9	condenser pressure	1.92	in.HgA
10	liquid enthalpy, Hf	67.8	BTU/lbm
11	vapor enthalph, Hg	1104.6	BTU/lbm
12	steam enthalpy	995.8	BTU/lbm
13	duty	2320	MBTU/hr
14	water outlet temperature	90.5	°F
15	LMTD	18.6	°F
16	UA	125.0	MBTU/hr/°F
17			
18	push to calculate		

9

The button updates the calculation using a simple bisection search algorithm, as indicated by the following VBA code:

```
Private Sub CommandButton1_Click()
    Dim iter As Integer, T1 As Double, T2 As Double, UA As
        Double
    UA = Worksheets("Sheet1").Range("AA6").Value
    T1 = Range("B14").Value
    T2 = 3 * Range("B14").Value - Range("B3").Value
    For iter = 1 To 32
        Range("B8").Value = (T1 + T2) / 2
        Calculate
        If (Range("B16").Value > UA) Then
            T1 = Range("B8").Value
        Else
            T2 = Range("B8").Value
        End If
    Next iter
End Sub
```

The second method can be found on the third tab, Sheet3. This is called *successive substitution*, or simply running the calculation over and over again, using the bivariate linear regression from the first tab. Excel will automatically solve this type of equation for you, provided you enable *iterative calculations*, as shown below:

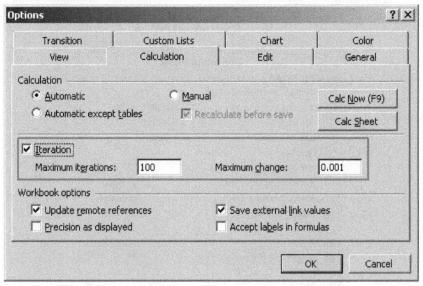

These are just two of many ways this component can be solved. Start with some reasonable estimate of the final result. Each iteration adjust this upward or downward based on the criterion, in this case the calculated vs. target UA. For this particular calculation (Equation 2.1) a higher value of Tsat will result in a lower calculated UA, so the direction of the adjustment must operate accordingly.

Air-Cooled Steam Surface Condensers

While these are very similar to the water-cooled variety, there are some differences. The curves may be provided in terms of how much steam can be condensed, rather than what pressure will be achieved, as in the following figure:

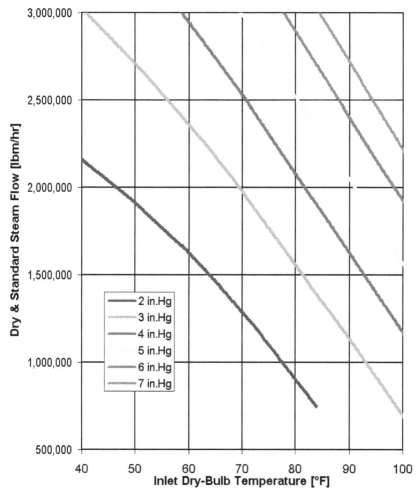

The auxiliary load (i.e., the power required to run the fans) is always a concern with air-cooled condensers. There is always motivation to run as few fans as required to meet some target operating pressure. That the performance varies with the number of fans means there is an additional variable to be considered. All of the data and regression details can be found in the spreadsheet air_cooled_condenser.xls in the same folder as before. Both LINEST and the solver are again used in the regression to best match the following presumed relationship:

$$Tsat=a+b*Tdb+c*duty+d*Psat+e/fans^f$$

LINEST determines the best values of a, b, c, d, and e; while the Solver determines the best value of f by minimizing the total residual in cell J6. The regression is shown in the following figure:

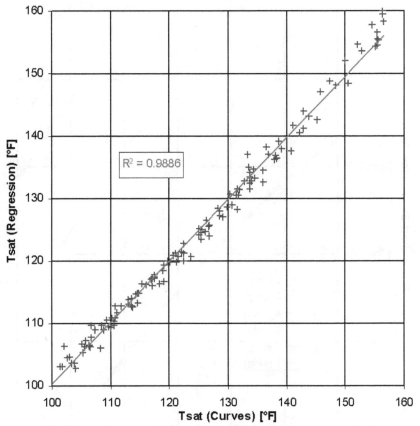

$R^2 = 0.9886$

We find the operating point using successive substitution on the second tabs. When Excel® is used to implement successive substitution, it is often necessary to use the intrinsic function IFERROR(calculation, estimate) to get it started with a reasonable numeric value.

	A	B	C
1	**Operating Point (successive substitution)**		
2	User Inputs		
3	ambient temperature	**89.7**	°F
4	fans on	**85%**	%
5	steam flow	**3,500,000**	lbm/hr
6	steam quality	**89.5%**	%
7	Calculations		
8	saturation temperature	123.2	°F
9	condenser pressure	3.77	in.HgA
10	liquid enthalpy, Hf	91.2	BTU/lbm
11	vapor enthalph, Hg	1114.6	BTU/lbm
12	steam enthalpy	1007.1	BTU/lbm
13	duty	3206	MBTU/hr
14	duty	92%	%

Push the button on the third tab (Sheet3) to see how rapidly successive substitution converges for this component for different starting values.

D	E	F	G	H	I	J	K	L
iteration	T1	T2	T3	T4	T5	T6	T7	T8
0	94.7	99.7	104.7	109.7	114.7	119.7	124.7	129.7
1	114.9	115.9	117.1	118.5	120.1	121.8	123.8	126.1
2	120.1	120.5	120.9	121.4	122.0	122.7	123.5	124.4
3	122.0	122.1	122.3	122.5	122.7	123.0	123.3	123.7
4	122.7	122.8	122.9	122.9	123.0	123.1	123.3	123.4
5	123.0	123.1	123.1	123.1	123.1	123.2	123.2	123.3
6	123.1	123.2	123.2	123.2	123.2	123.2	123.2	123.3
7	123.2	123.2	123.2	123.2	123.2	123.2	123.2	123.2
8	123.2	123.2	123.2	123.2	123.2	123.2	123.2	123.2
9	123.2	123.2	123.2	123.2	123.2	123.2	123.2	123.2
10	123.2	123.2	123.2	123.2	123.2	123.2	123.2	123.2
11	123.2	123.2	123.2	123.2	123.2	123.2	123.2	123.2
12	123.2	123.2	123.2	123.2	123.2	123.2	123.2	123.2
13	123.2	123.2	123.2	123.2	123.2	123.2	123.2	123.2
14	123.2	123.2	123.2	123.2	123.2	123.2	123.2	123.2
15	123.2	123.2	123.2	123.2	123.2	123.2	123.2	123.2
16	123.2	123.2	123.2	123.2	123.2	123.2	123.2	123.2
17	123.2	123.2	123.2	123.2	123.2	123.2	123.2	123.2
18	123.2	123.2	123.2	123.2	123.2	123.2	123.2	123.2
19	123.2	123.2	123.2	123.2	123.2	123.2	123.2	123.2
20	123.2	123.2	123.2	123.2	123.2	123.2	123.2	123.2

This next figure shows the same information in the table above, only in graphical form:

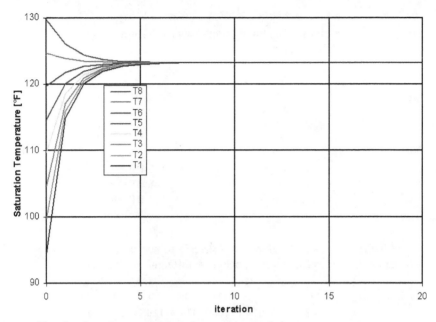

Clearly, there is no need for advanced methods here.

Chapter 3 Feedwater Heaters

Feedwater heaters are present in all regenerative Rankine cycle systems and are also sometimes used in various other cycles. These are *closed* heat exchangers, in that the hot and cold streams do not mix. Rankine cycles also have at least one *open* feedwater heater, which also serves the function of deaerator. We will cover those in Chapter 5. Feedwater heaters are most often of the following basic design:

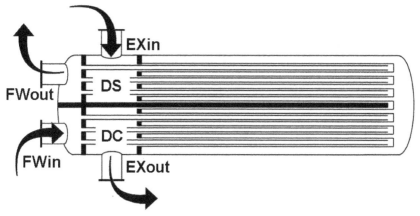

The cold feedwater enters the tube side at the bottom left and exits at the top left, after passing through a bank of U-tubes. The extraction steam enters at the top, condenses on the outside of the U-tubes, and drains at the bottom. A feedwater heater may or may not have a specially designed desuperheating section (DS) at the inlet and a drain cooler section (DC) at the bottom. Whether these sections contain extra baffles or a different arrangement is of interest from a design and fabrication standpoint, but the analysis is the same in any event.

If the steam enters superheated, it will be desuperheated, whether there's a special section to facilitate this or not. Likewise, the condensate leaving the drain will most likely be subcooled to some degree. In order to control the operation, some portion of the tubes must be flooded with condensate. As the heat transfer coefficient for condensation is greater than for the flooded section, it is desirable to maintain a minimum flooded section. In practice, the flooded fraction (or depth of flooding) can't be too small (or shallow); otherwise the liquid may completely drain during a transient event, triggering a vent.

While the steam path isn't exactly counterflow, baffles are used to force the steam to flow up and down along the U-tubes so as to roughly approximate counterflow. The end points are important in that the hottest steam is coincident with the hottest feedwater (i.e., top left) and the coldest condensate is coincident with the coldest feedwater (i.e. bottom left). The temperatures along the process path are illustrated in the following figure:

15

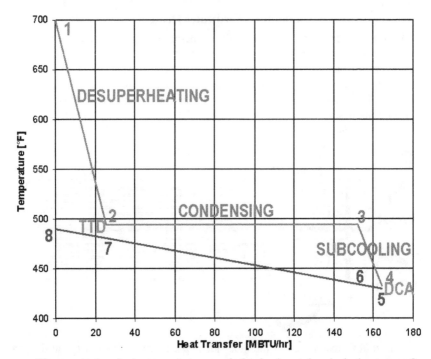

The vertical axis is temperature and the horizontal axis is heat transfer. Superheated steam enters at 1 and desuperheats until at 2 it becomes saturated vapor. The steam condenses from 2 to 3, where it becomes saturated liquid. The condensate is then subcooled from 3 to 4, where it drains out. The feedwater enters at 5 and exits at 8. The points 6 and 7 correspond to 3 and 2, respectively.

You cannot accurately model this process without splitting the heat exchanger up into three sections computationally. The NTU-effectiveness method will not accurately account for the entire process lumped together. If you split the heat exchanger up into three sections, the LMTD and NTU-effectiveness methods are identical in the case of steam, though there might be some slight difference with another working fluid if the feedwater specific heat varied considerably over the sections. The LMTD method is the correct way to analyze this type of heat exchanger.

The temperature difference between 4 and 5 is called the *drain cooler approach* (DCA). The temperature difference between 2 and 8 is called the *terminal temperature difference* (TTD). It is important to note that this is not *technically* the terminal temperature difference, as the two temperatures do not coincide (i.e., they are not at the same physical location) and 2 is not terminal (i.e., at the end of the path). This definition of TTD is unique to feedwater heaters in a Rankine cycle and must not be confused with the more general definition of a terminal difference. For this reason, the TTD may be zero and

16

even negative. Of course, this would not be thermodynamically possible if the two points were physically coincident. Needless to say, the difference between 1 and 8 will never be zero, let alone negative.

When solving a Rankine cycle, the feedwater flow, inlet pressure, inlet temperature, cold side pressure drop, steam inlet pressure, and enthalpy are generally known. The hot side pressure drop is also generally known and often presumed to be zero. If the TTD is specified and the DCA is also specified or that there is no subcooling at the drain, then the extraction steam flow can be calculated unambiguously.

$$\dot{m}_{feedwater}\left(h_8 - h_5\right) = \dot{m}_{steam}\left(h_1 - h_4\right) \qquad (3.1)$$

	A	B	C	D
1	**Typical Feedwater Heater**			97
2	User Inputs	value	units	
3	feedwater flow	2,500,000	lbm/hr	
4	feedwater inlet temp.	430.0	°F	T5
5	feedwater inlet pres.	3020	psia	
6	feedwater pres. drop	60	psi	
7	extraction steam temp.	700.0	°F	T1
8	extraction steam pres.	650	psia	
9	TTD	5.0	°F	
10	DCA	3.0	°F	
11	Calculations Group 1			
12	feedwater inlet enthalpy	410.4	BTU/lbm	
13	feedwater exit pressure	2960	psia	
14	saturation temperature	494.9	°F	T2,T3
15	feedwater exit temp.	489.9	°F	T8
16	feedwater exit enthalpy	476.1	BTU/lbm	
17	extraction enthalpy	1347.9	BTU/lbm	
18	drain temperature	433.0	°F	T4
19	drain enthalpy	411.4	BTU/lbm	
20	extraction flow	175,434	lbm/hr	
21	Calculations Group 2			
22	enthalpy of saturated vapor	1203.0	BTU/lbm	
23	enthalpy of saturated liquid	481.9	BTU/lbm	
24	Q desuperheating	25.4	MBTU/hr	
25	Q condensing	126.5	MBTU/hr	
26	Q subcooling	12.4	MBTU/hr	
27	FW enthalpy at 7	465.9	BTU/lbm	
28	FW temperature at 7	480.9	°F	T7
29	FW enthalpy at 6	415.3	BTU/lbm	
30	FW temperature at 6	434.6	°F	T6

These calculations can be found in the online archive in folder examples\ feedwater heater spreadsheet feedwater_heater.xls. Typical values are shown

17

above. When implementing a feedwater heater in a Rankine cycle, it is only necessary to assume some reasonable initial value and then update this each iteration with the solution of Equation 3.1. Again, no advanced methods are required and convergence will be achieved in less than a dozen iterations.

We next consider the internals of this component, that is, the thermal requirements to achieve some particular TTD and DCA. We note that the shell side heat transfer coefficient for condensation is largest, followed by liquid contact in the subcooling section, and finally vapor contact in the desuperheating section. These last two arise from the thermal conductivity of the liquid being significantly larger than the vapor phase. The heat transfer coefficient on the tube side is fairly uniform over the length of the tubes, making the shell side controlling. A typical value of U for steam in the condensing section is 600 BTU/hr/ft²/°F (3400 W/m²/°C). A typical value of U for steam in the subcooling section is 350 BTU/hr/ft²/°F (2000 W/m²/°C). A typical value of U for steam in the desuperheating section is 125 BTU/hr/ft²/°F (700 W/m²/°C). Based on these values we can estimate how much surface area is required. Calculations for each section are shown below:

31	Sections	DS	COND	SUB	units
32	heat transfer	25.4	126.5	12.4	MBTU/hr
33	overall h. t. coefficient, U	125	600	350	BTU/hr/ft²/°F
34	LMTD	72.5	31.8	19.1	°F
35	required area	2,806	6,634	1,849	ft²
36	total area			11,288	ft²

Here we see that 2,806 ft² of surface area is required to desuperheat the extraction steam, 6,635 ft² are required to condense, and 1,849 ft² are required to subcool. The total required surface area is 11,288 ft². This split (25%, 60%, 15%) is typical for this type of heat exchanger. This also means that 15% of the tube bundle will be flooded, which is adequate to maintain reasonable control over the extraction. Note that the control point will be the exit (i.e., there will be a level-actuated valve at the drain cooler outlet), rather than at the extraction steam inlet. Placing a valve at the inlet would result in an instability and continuous transients, which are undesirable.

18

Chapter 4. Moisture Separator Reheaters

A moisture separator reheater (MSR) combines two processes: 1) moisture removal (from wet steam) and 2) heating with extraction steam in order to further dry and slightly superheat the steam. These are used in nuclear steam systems because the reactor produces wet (or at best saturated) steam. The necessity of this process can be appreciated by considering the expansion of steam through a turbine on a Mollier chart (i.e., enthalpy vs. entropy diagram). Upon expansion, entropy increases because all real processes are irreversible and entropic (i.e., entropy-generating); thus, the process line extends to the right along the horizontal axis, while dropping enthalpy vertically. This takes the process through the steam dome into increasingly wet regions, which can damage the turbine. Consider the expansion line shown in the following figure:

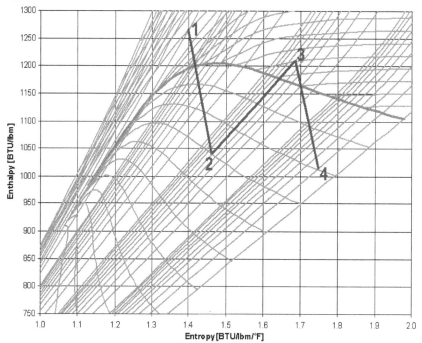

The red curve is the steam dome (i.e., 100% saturated vapor). Expansion from 1 to 2 ends at 70% quality (30% wet) and from 3 to 4 ends at 80% quality (20% wet). Expansion from 3 to 4 would not be possible but for moisture removal and heating from 2 to 3.

Computationally, a MSR is just a splitter and a heat exchanger. Most MSRs are two-stage. It is a simple matter to remove some fraction of the moisture along with some pressure drop and then reheat twice. With only slight

19

modifications, the same calculations used for feedwater heaters can be used to handle a MSR. Again, successive substitution of the either the extraction steam flows or the desired exit conditions will quickly converge to the final result. No advanced techniques are required. It is not necessary to solve any simultaneous nonlinear equations to implement a MSR, a fact that we will demonstrate subsequently. More on MSRs can be found in the reference, *Heat Exchangers*, listed in the preface.

Sample calculations can be found in the online archive in folder examples\MSR spreadsheet MSR.xls. An excerpt is shown below:

	A	B	C	D	E	F
1			**Moisture Separator Reheater Example**			
2	INPUTS	units	value	CALCS.	units	value
3	HP Tubes			LP Tubes		
4	Flow	lbm/hr	50,000	Tinlet	°F	443.7
5	Pinlet	psia	834.5	Toutlet	°F	438.7
6	Hinlet	BTU/lbm	1295.6	Houtlet	BTU/lbm	1054.9
7	Poutlet	psia	824.2	Shell Side		
8	Xoutlet	%	0.97	Tinlet	°F	370.8
9	LP Tubes			Xinlet	%	88.7%
10	Flow	lbm/hr	40,000	Tchevr	°F	369.2
11	Pinlet	psia	396.1	Xchevr	%	98.3%
12	Hinlet	BTU/lbm	1150.13	Hchevr	BTU/lbm	1181.7
13	Poutlet	psia	376.39	Hmidl	BTU/lbm	1189.3
14	Xoutlet	%	0.81	Tmidl	°F	368.7
15	Shell Side			Houtlet	BTU/lbm	1201.1
16	Flow	lbm/hr	500,000	Toutlet	°F	375.3
17	Pinlet	psia	175	superheat	°F	7.1
18	Hinlet	BTU/lbm	1100	LP Tubes		
19	chevrons	%	0.85	Q	BTU/hr	3.81E+06
20	Pchevr	psia	171.66	LMTD	°F	72.2
21	Poutlet	psia	169.43	FUA	BTU/hr/°F	5.27E+04
22	CALCS.	units	value	HP Tubes		
23	HP Tubes			Q	BTU/hr	5.87E+06
24	Tinlet	°F	638.9	LMTD	°F	69.2
25	Toutlet	°F	521.7	FUA	BTU/hr/°F	8.48E+04
26	Houtlet	BTU/lbm	1178.2	FUA total	BTU/hr/°F	1.38E+05
27						
28	user inputs in					
29	calculations in					

Chapter 5. Deaerators

Every recirculating vapor power system needs something to perform the function of a deaerator, even if there is no specific component referred to by this name. In a typical regenerative steam power system (i.e., Rankine cycle), the center feedwater heater is of the *open* variety (i.e., the hot and cold streams mix) and this is called a deaerator. In the steam tail (i.e., bottoming cycle) of a gas turbine combined power system, the deaerator is typically part of the low-pressure evaporator. The following is typical for such a device:

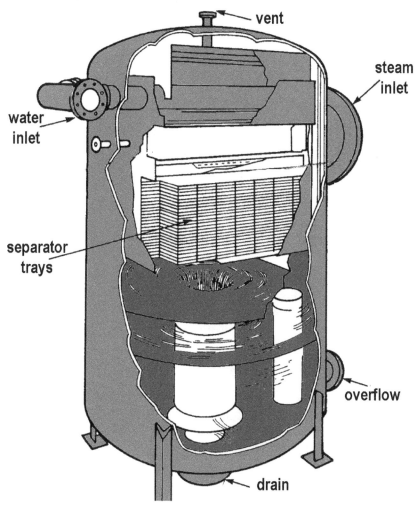

While there are many options for solving this particular component in GateCycle™, only one is meaningful: vary pressure with pegging steam, demand pegging steam. Here's how the device works: feedwater (compressed and subcooled liquid) enters through one port. Steam (may be superheated, saturated, or slightly wet) enters through a second port. Saturated liquid drains out of the bottom. The objective is to not have continuous venting, as this is an abnormal operation. The (pegging) steam is throttled to achieve a constant liquid level (demand pegging steam). The steam after throttling controls the pressure in the device (vary pressure with pegging steam). Any other computational option is meaningless and should never have been built into software in the first place. If some other option is available is available, don't use it.

Solution of the deaerator is quite simple and follows directly from the First Law of Thermodynamics (i.e., the conservation of mass and energy), as in the following equation:

$$\dot{m}_{feedwater}\, h_{feedwater} + \dot{m}_{steam}\, h_{steam} = \left(\dot{m}_{feedwater} + \dot{m}_{steam}\right) h_{sat.liq.} \quad (5.1)$$

which can be rearranged to yield the required steam flow:

$$\dot{m}_{steam} = \dot{m}_{feedwater}\, \frac{\left(h_{sat.liq.} - h_{feedwater}\right)}{\left(h_{steam} - h_{sat.liq.}\right)} \quad (5.2)$$

You will find a spreadsheet (deaerator.xls) in the folder examples\ deaerator in the free online archive. An excerpt appears below:

	A	B	C	D	E
1	Deaerator (Open FWH) Example			97	properties
2	INPUTS	units	value		
3	Feedwater				
4	flow	lbm/hr	350,000		
5	pressure	psia	1250		
6	temperature	°F	325		
7	Pegging Steam				
8	pressure	psia	400		
9	temperature	°F	500		
10	CALCULATIONS	units	value		
11	H feedwater	BTU/lbm	297.6		
12	H steam	BTU/lbm	1245.6		
13	T drain	°F	444.6		
14	H drain	BTU/lbm	424.2		
15	steam flow	lbm/hr	53,925		
16	user inputs in blue				
17	calculations in orange				

Chapter 6. Boilers and Steam Generators

Inside a thermodynamic cycle model, the function of a boiler or steam generator is simply that: heat up feed water. There may be some blow-down, leakage, and auxiliary flows. You will definitely need to account for pressure drop. There may be more than one stage or sections, including an economizer, evaporator, superheater, and reheater. These are not to be confused with combined cycle components having similar names. In this case, the heat comes from some fuel source or nuclear reactor, but not the exhaust of a gas turbine.

Do not attempt to analyze the fuel, air, or exhaust streams inside the Rankine cycle, as this is pointless—even counter-productive. GateCycle™ has a *fossil boiler* component. Don't use it. You will never have sufficient information to properly set-up such a component and you will derive no useful information by solving it. If you are running GateCycle™, always use the *aux boiler* component. You may need to account for the efficiency of the boiler. This information must come from sources outside the thermal cycle model, for example, from the manufacturer or an example from the test code. Boiler efficiency is not something you *get out* of a thermodynamic cycle model. It is something you *put into* one.

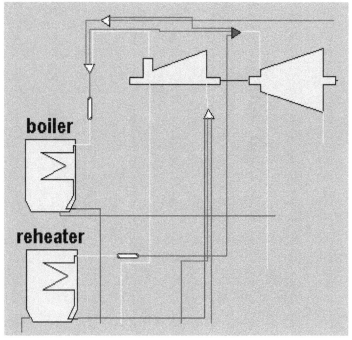

Solving this component is so trivial that we will not even give a simple example at this point.

Chapter 7. Pipes and Valves

Many thermodynamic cycle models have streams that change pressure and/or enthalpy. GateCycle™ streams do neither. Instead, there is a separate pipe component. All such models provide some sort of valve component. These typically control pressure (less than or equal to the inlet) and may lose heat, thus changing the enthalpy. Solution of these components is also trivial.

Chapter 8. Pumps

Most pumps come with curves, including head vs. flow and power vs. head and/or flow. I have never used a thermodynamic cycle modeling tool that readily accepted or facilitated the use of either one of these curves. This is not as unreasonable as it may seem. We are primarily interested in the impact of a pump *inside* the Rankine system. We don't care how much heat is lost to the environment by the pump or the electric motor driving it, nor do we care what the voltage or current are supplying the motor. These are all *external* to the Rankine cycle. What we are concerned with is increase in enthalpy across the pump, which accompanies a change in pressure and an increase in entropy.

The isentropic efficiency relates the enthalpies and this change.

$$\eta = \frac{\left(h_{2s} - h_1\right)}{\left(h_2 - h_1\right)} \tag{8.1}$$

Implementing this equation requires property calls SofTP and HofPS, which are included in the AllSteam Add-In.

It does matter whether the pump has the capacity to deliver a particular flow at the necessary pressure. I can recall three projects in the past decade that did not meet this requirement. In each case, I notified the owner's engineer during the testing phase that there might be a problem and, sure enough, there was. These instances are somewhat rare, as designers usually build in more than enough capacity with multiple pumps—not so much in other things, such as cooling towers, which rarely have any reserve capacity.

Chapter 9. Turbines

Steam turbines are complex machines, but not overly complicated to analyze in a Rankine cycle. The performance will vary with flow and inlet conditions and will be different for each stage and section. Unless you are working for a manufacturer, you will be supplied with this information, most often in the form of heat balances—that is, single operating points.

You may also be provided with PTC-6 correction curves. These are not particularly useful. Their purpose is to correct the results of a performance test, not provide expected performance at some operating point. The requirements of the performance test may not correspond to the normal operating conditions of the turbine, making the curves even less relevant to modeling a system with the turbine in it.

Aside from comical spaghetti curves for gas turbine performance created by novice (and really cheap) subcontractors, the most asinine curves I've ever seen were for Westinghouse nuclear steam turbine extraction enthalpies. The conditions at the exit of a steam turbine obviously depend on the inlet conditions as well as other factors. That is, if I were to somehow increase the steam inlet temperature by 100 degrees or the pressure by 20%, the exit enthalpy would not remain the same. Of course, these useless curves *presumed* constant inlet flow and conditions—something that never happens on this planet.

This is to say... you may or may not get any useful information from a steam turbine manufacturer. That's not to imply that they have no idea what they're doing. Westinghouse, for instance, made excellent steam turbines that have run quite reliably long beyond their expected lifetime. The quality of their pressurized water reactor steam system equipment is second to none. Still, their curves are garbage. There was a computer program called Syntha® that actually implemented such curves, not that I would recommend following this line of reasoning, but here's a link to their web site:

https://www.poweronline.com/doc/syntha-2000-v2-software-0001

There are only two parameters of interest here: 1) pressure and 2) isentropic efficiency. Besides directly specifying the pressures and efficiency via macros, the only option GateCycle™ has for modeling steam turbines is that of Spencer, Cotton, and Cannon.[14] SCC or some variant is almost always used.

Stodola's Law of the Ellipse

Steam turbine pressures were first successfully correlated by Stodola.[15] Upon plotting much data, Stodola found that the curves formed similar, that is a

---

[14] Spencer, R. C., Cotton, K. C., and Cannon, C. N.,"A Method for Predicting the Performance of Steam Turbine-Generators 16,500 kW and Larger," ASME Journal of Engineering for Power, Vol. 85, pp. 249–298, 1963.

[15] Stodola, A., *Steam and Gas Turbines*, McGraw-Hill, 1927.

conical sequence, of ellipses. The geometric shape led to an equation involving ratios of flow, temperature, and pressure, with the square root of the latter two quantities. After some simplifying assumptions (i.e., hand waving), the equation reduces to the ratio of flows being equal to the ratio of pressures. You can read more about this at:

https://en.wikipedia.org/wiki/Ellipse_Law

Thermodynamicists feel obligated to mention the work and equation of Stodola before moving on the actual calculations, which are: the pressure at the inlet of a steam turbine stage or section is roughly proportional to the flow exiting. In some cases you may need to make small adjustments, but this relationship is often all you have and may need.

Isentropic Efficiency

While it isn't immediately obvious from the SCC paper, nor clearly documented in the GateCycle™ help file, the way this works depends on which section you are modeling. The first (high pressure) section has a variable efficiency that is greatest at the design point and falls off on both sides (lower and higher flow). The intermediate or reheat section has the same efficiency regardless of the conditions, which is not realistic. The final (low pressure) section exhausting into a condenser has a linearly varying efficiency, which is also not realistic and can result in error messages when the efficiency is >100%.

$$\eta = \frac{(h_1 - h_2)}{(h_1 - h_{2S})} \tag{9.1}$$

Exhaust Losses

Steam turbine exhaust *loss* is a misnomer—a poor choice of words on the part of the late Ken Cotton, GE's steam turbine guru in the early years of the industry. Energy is not lost; rather, it transforms from one form to another and may become *unavailable*. This isn't the same as being *lost*. Cotton collected and analyzed a massive amount of data, applying numerous correlations so as to increase our understanding of these machines and processes. It just so happens that the impact of the exhausting conditions on the isentropic efficiency of a steam turbine is well correlated by calculating the average annulus velocity and correcting for moisture content. This brings us to the subject of expansion lines, a method of analysis and representation employed extensively by Ken Cotton. The simplest way to illustrate this concept is to plot these points on a *Mollier Chart* (i.e., an enthalpy-entropy diagram).

In the following figure, the thin violet curves are isobars (lines of constant pressure) and the thick blue segments are the expansion (steam process) lines. The points are in order, starting from the top left and continuing on to the bottom right. We will first consider the last two, which are labeled ELEP

(Expansion Line End Point) and UEEP (Ultimate Energy End Point). The UEEP is the actual total specific energy (in the form of enthalpy) that enters the condenser. This is the enthalpy that must be used to calculate the section gross (or shaft) power.

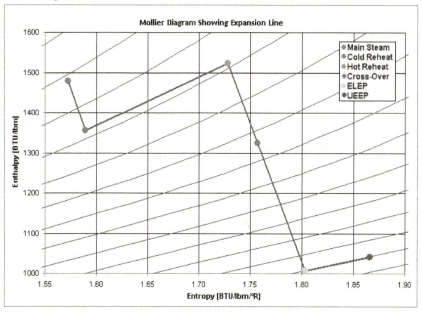

The ELEP doesn't physically exist and can't be measured. It is a fictitious state. The total specific energy is equal to the enthalpy plus the kinetic energy term, $V^2/2$. The velocity inside the steam turbine can't be directly measured and an appropriate average can't be determined. The velocity is known to be a substantial contribution to the total energy, but it is ignored in the *Exhaust Loss Method*, or rather the effect of it is "lumped" together in the *Exhaust Loss Correction*, which is used as an enthalpy adjustment. This can also be viewed as an efficiency correction.

The average (or *bulk*) steam velocity is used along with an *Exhaust Loss Curve* to arrive at an adjustment (or correction). Although the basis is vague and lacking in rigor, this method has proven to be quite successful-so much so that it is used throughout the industry worldwide and so it will be used here. The exhaust loss curve for the low pressure turbine in this example is shown in the following figure, along with the equations to be used in the calculation, including an adjustment for moisture. Curves similar to this are used throughout the industry. The calculation is given in the following figure in fine print next to the numeral 2 and also in the Equation below:

$$UEEP = ELEP + 0.87(1 - 0.01Y)ExhaustLoss \qquad (9.2)$$

31

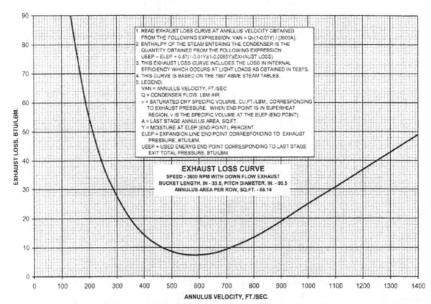

EXHAUST LOSS CURVE
SPEED - 3600 RPM WITH DOWN FLOW EXHAUST
BUCKET LENGTH, IN - 33.5, PITCH DIAMETER, IN. - 90.5
ANNULUS AREA PER ROW, SQ.FT. - 66.14

In the preceding equation, Y is the moisture (in percent) at the ELEP. Some manufacturers omit the 0.87, some the (1-0.01Y), and some both terms. Some manufacturers have annulus velocity on the horizontal axis and others have volumetric flow rate. Some state that the effective dry steam be used and others presume this, so check before you calculate. All such curves should have this same shape, that is, high (and unbounded) at low velocities, a minimum in the middle of the axis, and nearly linearly rising values with increasing velocities.

Sonic velocity in steam at these conditions is roughly 1400 ft/sec (427 m/s). A shock will occur as the velocity approaches this value, which can result in catastrophic damage. The turbine should not be operated in these conditions; therefore, the calculation should not be performed either. Keep this in mind when modeling these systems. It is customary to *clamp* the velocity at sonic and presume that it cannot exceed this value. In practice, operators should turn off fans in the cooling tower or air-cooled condenser and/or shut down circulating water pumps to avoid this condition. Besides the potential for turbine blade and condenser tube damage, the efficiency is lower under these conditions plus shutting off fans or pumps will also reduce auxiliary load.

Chapter 10. Generators

The following are typical generator loss curves:

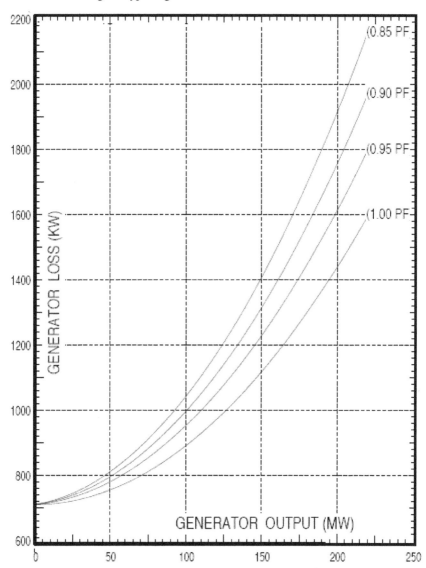

If at all possible, insist on curves from the manufacturer that look like this. While you can use efficiency curves, such as appear on the next page, loss curves are more accurate and useful. Phase curves that look like a spider web are useless for inferring generator losses.

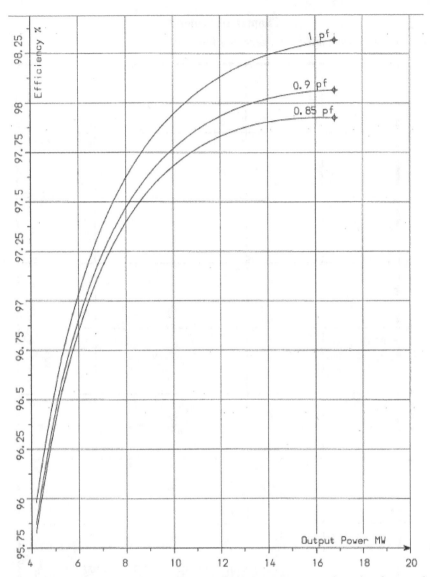

Such curves can be readily digitized, for instance using the free tool available at my web site:

https://dudleybenton.altervista.org/software/Digitize215.zip

The results are automatically copied onto the clipboard and will paste directly into Excel®. The spreadsheet (generator.xls) is in the folder examples\ generator. All of the curves will collapse to a single curve having the form:

34

$$Losses = function\left(\frac{output}{PF^n}\right) \qquad (10.1)$$

A simple quadratic or cubic will be adequate. We use the Excel® function LINEST to determine the coefficients. There is a convenient shortcut notation for powers of x: =LINEST(C3:C116,D3:D116^{1,2,3},TRUE,TRUE). The ^{1,2,3} saves creating separate columns for x, x^2, and x^3. Use the Excel® Solver to determine the optimum exponent, n, (cell D2) by minimizing the total residual, which is in cell G6. This is what the spreadsheet looks like:

	A	B	C	D	E	F	G	H	I
1	Typical Generator Curves						LINEST		
2	PF	MW	Loss	1.58	fit	-8.7E-06	0.020572	-0.04285	716.0933
3	1.00	2	709	2	716	3.69E-06	0.001565	0.191214	6.506094
4	1.00	16	714	16	721	0.9983	15.86039	#N/A	#N/A
5	1.00	30	726	30	733	21537.64	110	#N/A	#N/A
6	1.00	40	740	40	746	16253514	27670.73	#N/A	#N/A
7	1.00	54	763	54	772				
8	1.00	62	780	62	791				
9	1.00	70	800	70	812				
10	1.00	79	820	79	838				
11	1.00	86	846	86	860				
12	1.00	98	883	98	902				
13	1.00	105	911	105	930				

The combined correlation is quite good:

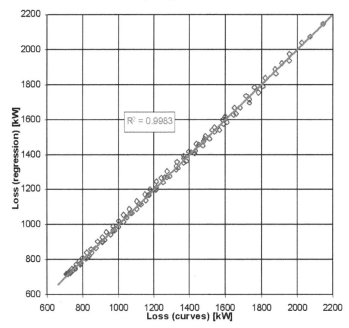

If the curves don't collapse to a single curve with an exponent between 0.5 and 2.5, there's something wrong with the curves. The exponent should be closer to 1.5. The regression curves should be adequate, as shown in this next figure:

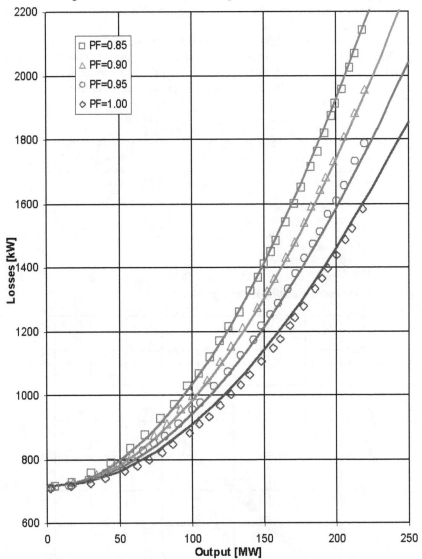

The regression efficiency curves are:

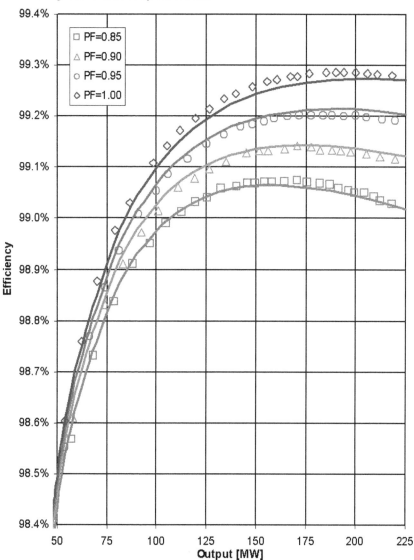

37

Chapter 11. Solving Rankine Cycle Systems

We now have all of the parts of a conventional Rankine cycle and so we will consider several solutions, beginning with the simplest. You will find all of the files in the folder examples/cycle1, including: an Excel® spreadsheet plus all of the GateCycle™ input and output files. The system is shown in the following figure:

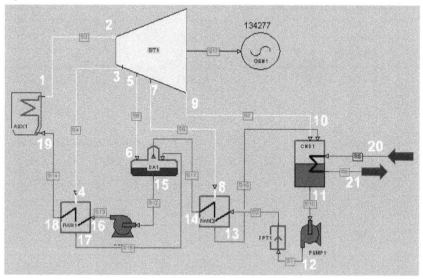

This is the step-by-step procedure for solving this cycle. Boiler exit conditions (pressure, temperature, and flow) are prescribed (point 1). You may want to allow for some pressure drop and enthalpy loss between points 1 and 2. After performing this step, the inlet conditions to the turbine are known. You must assume pressures at points 3, 5, 7, and 10. There is no pressure drop or enthalpy loss between points 9 and 10. You must also assume a flow at points 4, 6, and 8.

You know the isentropic efficiency of each stage of the steam turbine and also the exhaust loss curve. Use Equations 9.1 and 9.2 to calculate the properties at points 3, 5, 7, 9 (and 10). There may be pressure drop and heat loss between points 3 and 4, 5 and 6, 7 and 8. Apply these and move on.

The properties at point 11 are known from the pressure you assumed at points 9 (or 10). Calculate the properties at 12 using Equation 8.1 and then move to points 13 and 14. Use the equations in Chapter 3 to calculate the properties at point 14 and then in Chapter 5 for point 15. Again Equation 8.1 to obtain point 16 and Chapter 3 to obtain points 17 and 18. Use Chapter 6 for the boiler and the cycle is complete.

Now for the first round of iterative corrections. Chapter 3 explains how to adjust the flows at 3 and 7. Chapter 5 explains how to adjust the flow at 5.

Chapter 2 explains how to adjust the pressure at 9 (or 10). Chapter 9 explains how to adjust the pressures at 3, 5, and 7 plus either the pressure at 2 to match the flow at 1 or the flow at 1 to match the pressure at 2. Repeat this process a dozen times and it will converge. Calculate the generator losses and you're done. The details are in the spreadsheet.

	A	B	C	D	E	F	G	H
1	**Typical Steam System**		flow	P	T	H	S	X
2	cycle points	#	kg/s	kPa	°C	kJ/kg	kJ/kg/°K	quality
3	boiler exit	1	125.0	12636	535.0	3436	6.577	VAP
4	turbine inlet	2	125.0	12004	531.4	3433	6.596	VAP
5	1st extr. at turbine	3	15.4	1734	262.7	2945	6.688	VAP
6	1st extr. at heater	4	15.4	1647	260.9	2944	6.708	VAP
7	2nd extr. at turbine	5	11.6	246	126.9	2602	1.602	95%
8	2nd extr. at deaerator	6	11.6	234	125.2	2601	1.584	95%
9	3rd extr. at turbine	7	5.6	35.7	73.1	2334	7.708	87%
10	3rd extr. at heater	8	5.6	33.9	71.9	2333	7.726	87%
11	expansion line end point	9	92.4	5.46	34.5	2120	8.362	82%
12	used energy end point	10	92.4	5.46	34.5	2132	6.785	82%
13	condensate	11	98.0	5.46	34.5	144	0.498	0%
14	heater 3 inlet	12	98.0	1750	34.6	146	0.499	LQD
15	heater 3 drain	13	5.6	34	47.1	197	0.666	LQD
16	heater 3 exit	14	98.0	1575	64.4	271	0.885	LQD
17	deaerator drain	15	125.0	234	125.2	526	1.584	0%
18	heater 1 inlet	16	125.0	17387	127.5	547	1.592	LQD
19	heater 1 drain	17	15.4	1647	140.0	590	1.738	LQD
20	heater 1 exit	18	125.0	15648	195.3	838	2.265	LQD
21	boiler inlet	19	125.0	14866	195.1	837	2.265	LQD
22	cooling water inlet	20	3500	350	15.0	63	0.224	LQD
23	cooling water exit	21	3500	315	28.0	118	0.409	LQD
24	turbine exit calculations	units						
25	ELEP	kJ/kg	2120					
26	quality at ELEP	%	81.7%					
27	density at ELEP	kg/m³	0.047					
28	annulus velocity	m/s	196					
29	uncorrected exh. loss	kJ/kg	19.6					
30	corrected exhaust loss	kJ/kg	12.2	note: this moisture correction can be f(				
31	UEEP	kJ/kg	2132					
32	condenser calculations	units						
33	heat load	MWt	190.6					
34	temperature rise	°C	13.0					
35	saturation temperature	°C	34.5					
36	saturation pressure	kPa	5.46					

Change any of the bold blue numbers and push the button to solve the system.

37	pressure losses		
38	boiler	15%	
39	main steam line	5%	
40	1st extraction line	5%	
41	2nd extraction line	5%	
42	3rd extraction line	5%	
43	heater 1	10%	
44	heater 3	10%	
45	feedwater	5%	
46	cooling water	10%	
47	enthalpy losses	kJ/kg	
48	main steam	2.5	
49	1st extraction line	1.0	
50	2nd extraction line	1.0	
51	3rd extraction line	1.0	
52	feed water	1.0	
53	efficiencies		
54	turbine efficiency	91.0%	see turbine tab for curve
55	condensate pump eff.	85%	
56	main feed pump eff.	85%	
57	terminal temp. differ.	°C	
58	heater 1	7.5	
59	heater 3	7.5	
60	drain cooler approach	°C	
61	heater 1	12.5	
62	heater 3	12.5	
63	boiler calculations	units	
64	net heat input	MWt	324.9
65	efficiency	86.9%	see boiler tab
66	gross heat input	MWt	373.9
67	turbine calculations	units	
68	stage 1 power	MWe	61.0
69	stage 2 power	MWe	37.6
70	stage 3 power	MWe	26.2
71	stage 4 power	MWe	18.7
72	total shaft power	MWe	143.6
73	power factor	-	0.85
74	generator losses	MWe	3.0
75	generator output	MWe	140.6
76	heat rate	kJ/kWh	9575

There are several tabs. One has the boiler curve, another has the generator curves, a third has the condenser curves, and a fourth has the steam turbine curves. The bold blue numbers on each tab are user inputs and feed back into the main tab to impact the cycle. If you happen to have a copy of GateCycle™ there even a tab for that. Everything is contained in this one spreadsheet.

NO SIMULTANEOUS
NONLINEAR EQUATIONS
SOLVED WHATSOEVER!

I can't emphasize strongly enough that at no point in this process were any simultaneous nonlinear equations solved. You could represent this cycle as a system of simultaneous nonlinear equations, but it is completely unnecessary and extremely wasteful to do so. I have been asked on several occasions what nonlinear constrained minimization method or MatLab® function or Python® library routine or other such elaborate procedure or extreme measure is required to solve a Rankine or gas turbine combined cycle. I anticipate some day being asked what genetic algorithm or artificial intelligence or alien technology is required to accomplish this simple and straightforward task. These questions assume that a billion-dollar singing robot is needed to open a can of soda, when all that's required is to pull the tab.

Instead, let us consider the C code required to solve this simple system. Both English and SI versions are provided in separate folders beneath cycle1. First, the user-defined parameters that define system performance:

```
int year=97; /* steam properties (must be 67, 69, 84,
    95, or 97) */

double Aarea=108.; /* annulus area in [ft^2] */

/* user-defined turbine flow factors (pressure/flow) */

double ff1=0.00171000;
double ff2=0.00028500;
double ff3=0.00004250;
double ff4=0.00000675;

/* user-defined pressure drops */

double dPbo=0.15;
double dP12=0.05;
double dP34=0.05;
double dP56=0.05;
double dP78=0.05;

/* user-defined enthalpy drops [kJ/kg] */

double dH12=1.0;
double dH34=0.5;
double dH56=0.5;
double dH78=0.5;
```

```
/* user-defined heater variables */

double TTD1=10.;
double TTD3=10.;
double DCA1= 5.;
double DCA3= 5.;
```

The generator, boiler, and turbine curves are implemented as functions:

```
/* user-defined performance functions */

double GenLoss(double kWnet,double PF)
{
double x;
x=kWnet/pow(150000.,1.5);
return((1500.*x-65.)*x+850.);
}

double BlrEff(double pph)
{
double x;
x=pph/2.204622622/3600./115.;
return((((-0.794407*x+1.84942)*x-
1.68)*x+1.04333)*x+0.453681);
}

double STeff(double flow) /* could have different
    efficiency for each section */
{
double x;
x=flow/2.204622622/3600.;
return(((-8.288101141E-7*x+0.0001991260511)*x-
0.01082475795)*x+0.7701450149);
}

double Exloss(double fps) /* exhaust loss in [BTU/lbm]
    */
{
return(((((0.095908075*fps-
108.1160204)*fps+38062.85256)*fps-
1784140.38)/fps/fps);
}
```

The turbine, pump, feedwater heater, and deaerator procedures are the same for any Rankine cycle:

```
/* generic cycle functions (not specific to any
    particular system) */

void Turbine(double P1,double H1,double P2,double
    efficiency,double*H2)
{
```

43

```
double H2S,S1;
S1=SofPH(P1,H1,year);
H2S=HofPS(P2,S1,year);
*H2=H1+(H2S-H1)*efficiency;
}

void Pump(double P1,double H1,double P2,double
    efficiency,double*H2)
{
double H2S,S1;
S1=SofPH(P1,H1,year);
H2S=HofPS(P2,S1,year);
*H2=H1+(H2S-H1)/efficiency;
}

void FWH(double F5,double P5,double H5,double P1,double
    H1,double TTD,double
    DCA,double*F1,double*H4,double*H8)
{
double T4,T5,T8,Ts;
T5=TofPH(P5,H5,year);
Ts=Tsat(P1,year);
T4=T5+DCA;
*H4=HofTP(T4,P1,year);
T8=Ts-TTD;
*H8=HofTP(T8,P5,year);
*F1=F5*(*H8-H5)/(H1-*H4);
}

void Deaerator(double Ffw,double Hfw,double Pex,double
    Hex,double*Fex,double*Hdr)
{
double Ts;
Ts=Tsat(Pex,year);
*Hdr=Hf(Ts,year);
*Fex=Ffw*(*Hdr-Hfw)/(Hex-*Hdr);
}
```

The cycle solver is also straightforward:

```
void SolveCycle(double F1,double T1,double F20,double
    T20,double PF)
{
int converged,iter;
double F3,F4,F5,F6,F7,F8,F9,F11;
double
    H1,H2,H3,H4,H5,H6,H7,H8,H9,H10,H11,H12,H13,H14,H15,H1
    6,H17,H18;
double P1,P2,P3,P4,P5,P6,P7,P8,P9,P10,P12,P16;
double T2,T4,T6,T8;
double c2,c3,c5,c7,kWgross,kWnet,Qgross,Qnet,Van;
```

```
printf("F1=%.0lf, T1=%.1lf, F20=%.0lf, T20=%.0lf,
  PF=%.3lf\n",F1,T1,F20,T20,PF);

/* initialize implicit variables */

P1=1800.;
P3=250.;
P5=35.;
P7=5.;
P9=0.8122;
F3=0.12*F1;
F5=0.08*F1;
F7=0.04*F1;

/* iteratively solve system */

printf("it    F3  /  F4      F5 /  F6      F7 / F8
  P9 /  P10\n");
for(iter=0;iter<32;iter++)
  {
  H1=HofTP(T1,P1,year); /* boiler exit */
  P2=P1*(1.-dP12); /* main steam at turbine */
  H2=H1-dH12;
  T2=TofPH(P2,H2,year);
  Turbine(P2,H2,P3,STeff(F1),&H3); /* first stage */
  Turbine(P3,H3,P5,STeff(F1),&H5); /* second stage */
  Turbine(P5,H5,P7,STeff(F1),&H7); /* third stage */
  Turbine(P7,H7,P9,STeff(F1),&H9); /* ELEP [BTU/lbm]
  */
  F9=F1-F3-F5-F7;
  Van=AnnulusVelocity(F9,P9,H9); /* annulus velocity
  [ft/sec] */
  H10=H9+Exloss(Van); /* UEEP [BTU/lbm] */
  P4=P3*(1.-dP34);
  H4=H3-dH34;
  T4=TofPH(P4,H4,year); /* 1st extraction */
  P6=P5*(1.-dP56);
  H6=H5-dH56;
  T6=TofPH(P6,H6,year); /* 2nd extraction */
  P8=P7*(1.-dP78);
  H8=H7-dH78;
  T8=TofPH(P8,H8,year); /* 3rd extraction */
  H11=Hf(Tsat(P9,year),year); /* condensate */
  F11=F9+F7;
  P12=P5*1.5;
  Pump(P9,H11,P12,0.75,&H12); /* pump */
  FWH(F11,P12,H12,P8,H8,TTD3,DCA3,&F8,&H13,&H14); /*
  FWH3 */
```

45

```
   Deaerator(F11,H14,P6,H6,&F6,&H15);  /* deaerator */
   P16=P1/(1.-dPbo);
   Pump(P6,H15,P16,0.65,&H16);  /* pump */
   FWH(F1,P16,H16,P4,H4,TTD1,DCA1,&F4,&H17,&H18);  /*
   FWH1 */
   P10=Pcond(F8*(H13-H11)+F9*(H10-H11),T20);

/* check for convergence and exit loop or update and
   continue */

   printf("%2i %6.0lf/%6.0lf %6.0lf/%6.0lf
   %5.0lf/%5.0lf
   %6.4lf/%6.4lf\n",iter,F4,F3,F6,F5,F8,F7,P10,P9);
   converged=1;
   if(fabs(F4/F3-1.)>0.00001)converged=0;
   if(fabs(F6/F5-1.)>0.00001)converged=0;
   if(fabs(F8/F7-1.)>0.00001)converged=0;
   if(fabs(P10/P9-1.)>0.00001)converged=0;
   c2=ff1*F1;
   c3=ff2*(F1-F3);
   c5=ff3*(F1-F3-F5);
   c7=ff4*(F1-F3-F5-F7);
   if(fabs(P2/c2-1.)>0.00001)converged=0;
   if(fabs(P3/c3-1.)>0.00001)converged=0;
   if(fabs(P5/c5-1.)>0.00001)converged=0;
   if(fabs(P7/c7-1.)>0.00001)converged=0;
   if(converged)
     break;
   F3=F4;
   F5=F6;
   F7=F8;
   P9=P10;
   P1=c2/(1.-dP12);
   P3=c3;
   P5=c5;
   P7=c7;
   }

/* generator output and losses */

   kWgross=(F1*(H2-H3)+(F1-F3)*(H3-H5)+(F1-F3-F5)*(H5-
   H7)+(F1-F3-F5-F7)*(H7-H10))/3412.141633;
   kWnet=kWgross;
   for(iter=0;iter<5;iter++)
   kWnet=kWgross-GenLoss(kWnet,PF);

/* boiler efficiency and heat input */

   Qnet=F1*(H1-H18);
```

46

```
Qgross=Qnet/BlrEff(F1);
printf("kWnet=%.01f, Qgross=%.21E\n",kWnet,Qgross);
}
```
Typical program output is listed below:

```
F1=750000, T1=1050.0, F20=7750000, T20=60, PF=0.900
it  F3  / F4     F5 / F6      F7 / F8      P9 / P10
 0 89374/90000 68218/60000 33449/30000 0.6525/0.8122
 1 83509/89374 61168/68218 30307/33449 0.6521/0.6525
 2 83987/83509 62555/61168 30536/30307 0.6689/0.6521
 3 83719/83987 62394/62555 30623/30536 0.6667/0.6689
 4 83786/83719 62424/62394 30622/30623 0.6671/0.6667
 5 83782/83786 62423/62424 30624/30622 0.6670/0.6671
 6 83783/83782 62422/62423 30620/30624 0.6670/0.6670
 7 83783/83783 62422/62422 30620/30620 0.6670/0.6670
kWnet=104398, Qgross=1.06E9
```

The iterations usually converge in less than 8 iterations. You can specify which steam properties (i.e., IAPWS-IF67, KKHM, NBS/NRC, IAPWS-SF95, or IAPWS-IF97) to use as an optional command argument (i.e., 67, 69, 84, 95, or 97). The main program contains a loop to run 480 cases. How long each takes depends strongly on which steam properties you select, as listed in the following table:

cycle1 times - English units

year	cases	time	sec/case
67	480	88.050	0.1834
69	480	287.900	0.5998
84	480	486.213	1.0129
95	480	628.463	1.3093
97	480	5.541	0.0115

The *scientific* formulations (based on T,ρ) are considerably more time-consuming than the *industrial* formulations (based on T,P). The slowest is SF95, which takes 113 times as long as the IF97. The motivation for these industrial formulations is then clear. Even further improvement in speed could be achieved by developing formulations in terms of P,H and P,S. With the IF97 requiring a little more than 1/100th of a second, there is little motivation to do so.

We can get details on each function call using the Digital Mars compiler (see Appendix B). This will further explain exactly which functions are time-consuming and why. The following table lists each function, how many times it is called to complete one cycle solution, how many seconds elapsed while inside the function, and how many seconds per call. The far right column lists the AllSteam function which calls the formulation specific one. In this case the 1969 KKHM formulation was used.

47

cycle1 function calls and times

Num Calls	Func Time	Func Time	Per Call	function name	related function
6410	28.919	23.57%	0.004	P69	PofTV
7443	15.650	12.76%	0.002	fQ	
7058	14.676	11.96%	0.002	fQr	
224	14.170	11.55%	0.063	Tsat69	Tsat
1049	8.457	6.89%	0.008	R69	VofTP
8602	7.225	5.89%	0.000	Psat69	Psat
648	6.892	5.62%	0.010	H69	HofTV
494	6.230	5.08%	0.012	rhof	Vf
391	3.312	2.70%	0.008	rhog	Vg
385	2.440	1.99%	0.006	S69	SofTV
1033	2.010	1.64%	0.001	fQt	
344	1.527	1.24%	0.004	_HofTP	HofTP
1	1.131	0.92%	1.131	SolveCycle	
64	1.067	0.87%	0.016	_TofPH	TofPH
24	0.940	0.77%	0.039	_TofPS	TofPS
1033	0.836	0.68%	0.000	fAt	
177	0.779	0.63%	0.004	_SofTP	SofTP
160	0.724	0.59%	0.004	_Hf	Hf
144	0.629	0.51%	0.004	_Hg	Hg
48	0.601	0.49%	0.012	_SofPH	SofPH
48	0.576	0.47%	0.012	_HofPS	HofPS
224	0.541	0.44%	0.002	_Tsat	Tsat
648	0.527	0.43%	0.000	fA	
192	0.476	0.39%	0.002	_Psat	
104	0.462	0.38%	0.004	_Sf	
104	0.454	0.37%	0.004	_Sg	
16	0.211	0.17%	0.013	FWH	
32	0.137	0.11%	0.004	Turbine	
48	0.131	0.11%	0.002	SofPH	
48	0.120	0.10%	0.002	HofPS	
48	0.113	0.09%	0.002	TofPH	
40	0.107	0.09%	0.002	HofTP	
40	0.096	0.08%	0.002	Tsat	
8	0.079	0.06%	0.009	density	

cycle1 function calls and times continued

Num Calls	Func Time	Func Time	Per Call	function name	related function
16	0.067	0.05%	0.004	Pump	
24	0.058	0.05%	0.002	Hf	
113	0.055	0.04%	0.000	fmax	
113	0.051	0.04%	0.000	fmin	
1	0.037	0.03%	0.037	main	
8	0.034	0.03%	0.004	Deaerator	
8	0.020	0.02%	0.002	Vg	
8	0.020	0.02%	0.002	AnnulusVelocity	
8	0.020	0.02%	0.002	Hg	
8	0.019	0.02%	0.002	Pcond	
8	0.019	0.02%	0.002	Psat	
8	0.018	0.01%	0.002	Vf	
32	0.016	0.01%	0.000	STeff	
8	0.005	0.00%	0.000	Exloss	
5	0.005	0.00%	0.001	GenLoss	
1	0.000	0.00%	0.000	BlrEff	
37701	122.689	100.00%	1.450	totals	

We see from this table that 23.57% of the entire time was consumed calling PofTV to find the specific volume (or density) corresponding to a particular pressure and temperature. The partition function (fQ) and its partial derivative with respect to density (fQr) and temperature (fQt) consumed 12.76%, 11.96%, and 1.64%, respectively, totaling 26.36%. This is not surprising, considering there were a total of 6410, 7443, 7058, and 1033, respectively, to these functions. The remaining functions consumed the other 50.07%. In fact, property calls accounted for 98.56% of the total time. All of the functions inside cycle1.c combined accounted for a mere 1.44% of the runtime. This is typical for this type of program.

With only minor modifications, the preceding code (cycle1.c) is converted to SI units. You will find this, along with the associated files, in folder examples \cycle1\SI. Typical output is similar to the previous and the runtime is the same.

```
F1=125.0, T1=850.0, F20=3500, T20=35, PF=1.000
it   F3 /  F4     F5 / F6     F7 / F8      P9  /   P10
 0 14.99/15.00 11.59/10.00  5.81/ 5.00 0.005629/0.006000
 1 15.02/14.99 11.35/11.59  6.00/ 5.81 0.005629/0.005629
 2 15.12/15.02 11.39/11.35  5.91/ 6.00 0.005629/0.005629
 3 15.11/15.12 11.38/11.39  5.90/ 5.91 0.005629/0.005629
```

49

```
4 15.11/15.11 11.38/11.38   5.90/ 5.90 0.005629/0.005629
5 15.11/15.11 11.38/11.38   5.90/ 5.90 0.005629/0.005629
6 15.11/15.11 11.38/11.38   5.90/ 5.90 0.005629/0.005629
7 15.11/15.11 11.38/11.38   5.90/ 5.90 0.005629/0.005629
8 15.11/15.11 11.38/11.38   5.90/ 5.90 0.005629/0.005629
kWnet=139188, Qgross=387767, HtRt=10029
784 cases in 6.103 seconds
```

This program (cycle1.c) is very specific in that it only handles a single configuration. QUEST is a much more versatile program that can handle most conventional coal-fired or oil-fired steam power systems. QUEST is described in Appendix C and is also available free on my web site.

Chapter 12. Gas Turbines

Gas turbines are rarely solved in the true sense within a cycle model such as GateCycle™ or ThermoFlow™. While GateCycle™ is capable of doing this at some level using individual components (compressor, combustor, expander, and generator), you are not likely to have enough information on these components to build a realistic model. GateCycle™ can work with a compressor map, but it's a real mess. Even the variables are vague and distorted (e.g., normalized pressure ratios and efficiencies). I do not recommend attempting it.

The way gas turbines are modeled is with correction curves provided by the manufacturer. Most manufacturers are quite proud of their products and are pleased to supply you with such information on request. After all, they're in the business of selling engines and are always looking for customers. One common engine is the General Electric LM6000 model PF25. You will find the correction curves for this engine in the examples\gas turbines folder in spreadsheet LM6000 PF25 Correction Curves.xls. These follow the guidance of ASME PTC-22 (2005).

Correction Curve Methodology

The correction curve methodology *presumes* that the impact of various ambient and operating conditions are *small adjustments* made to a larger whole and are mostly independent of each other. Of course, this is not strictly true, but the industry uses it anyway. If these adjustments (i.e., corrections) are small, then they can be applied sequentially, either multiplicatively or additively to the base performance to obtain the expected performance at some other conditions. Most of the time this works fairly well, though this calculation can yield inaccurate results.

GateCycle™ makes no check whatsoever on the reasonableness of such corrections. For instance, you can specify a power multiplier of 2, 10, or 1000, as well as a fuel consumption multiplier of 0.1, 0.01, or 0.001, yielding an absurd heat rate (i.e., efficiency). This won't happen if you use the individual components, but that path has its own problems.

You will always need ambient temperature, barometric pressure, and relative humidity corrections. You will often need fuel temperature and composition corrections. For each of these conditions, you will need a correction for power, heat rate, exhaust flow, and exhaust temperature. Most often, the first three are multiplicative and the last (exhaust temperature) is additive. Sixteen of these are provided in the spreadsheet. Each one is graphed individually and is typical for the industry. Two of these appear on the following page: power and exhaust flow vs. ambient dry-bulb temperature.

You will notice that both of these exhibit a discontinuity at around 45°F. This jump in performance results from the activation of spray intercooling technology (called SPRINT™ by G.E.), which is a performance enhancement process available with some models and under some operating conditions. You will need to consider such things in your cycle model.

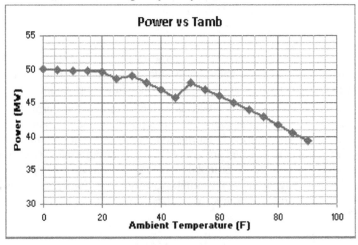

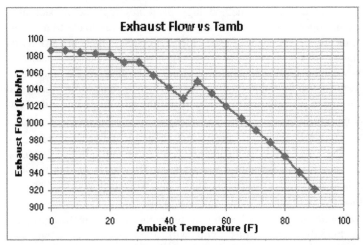

The calculations are implemented in cells U1:Y11 on the second tab of the spreadsheet. In this case, the corrections are generated from performance runs (cells A3:O75) by either dividing or subtracting from the reference performance (cells A43:O43) to obtain multiplicative or additive factors, respectively (cells P3:P75). These factors are applied using linear interpolation (supplied as a macro). Splines and curve-fits are often used as well. These corrections are input to GateCycle™ in the form of tables, which can be either linearly interpolated or splined. If there is a discontinuity, as in this case, beware of splines because they can exaggerate the transition region of the curves.

52

	U	V	W	X	Y
1		Sample Implementation			
2		Conditions			
3	baro	Tdb	RH		
4	14.51	73.2	86%		
5		Corrections			
6	baro	0.9871	1.0004	0.9871	0.3
7	Tdb	0.9379	1.0131	0.9601	7.3
8	RH	1.0017	1.0004	0.9986	1.0
9		Results			
10		kW	BTU/kWh	EGW	EGT
11		43,324	8,415	979,024	865.3

This spreadsheet also contains corrections for inlet and exhaust pressure drop. Inlet pressure drop occurs across the filter and conditioning, if any, which may be an evaporative cooler, fogger, or chiller. The exhaust pressure drop occurs across the Heat Recovery Steam Generator (HRSG) or other exhaust device. A very simple implementation would be (You can find this code snippet in examples\CCPP\CCPP1.c):

```
typedef struct{double kWnet,kJkWh,EGW,EGT;}GT;

GT LM6000={46720,   /* net power output [kW] */
            8757,   /* net heat rate [kJ/kWh] */
             300,   /* exhaust flow [kg/s] */
             730};  /* exhaust temperature [deg K] */

GT GasTurbinePerformance(double P,double T,double RH)
  {
   static GT gt;
   gt.kWnet=LM6000.kWnet    *(P/0.101325)
 *(-0.00433*(T-286.)+1.)*( 0.00655*(RH-0.6)+1.);
   gt.kJkWh=LM6000.kJkWh    *(0.101325/P)
 *( 0.00127*(T-286.)+1.)*( 0.00153*(RH-0.6)+1.);
   gt.EGW  =LM6000.EGW      *(P/0.101325)
 *(-0.00310*(T-286.)+1.)*(-0.00533*(RH-0.6)+1.);
   gt.EGT  =LM6000.EGT+132.3*(P-0.101325)
 +  0.489  *(T-286.)    +  2.39  *(RH-0.6)    ;
   return(gt);
  }
```

Exhaust Composition

While the exhaust flow and temperature can be arbitrarily controlled with such curves, either through multiplication or addition, the exhaust composition is another problem altogether. The exhaust composition is required because the specific heat depends on it. That is, it matters how much water vapor and carbon dioxide is in the exhaust, as both of these gases have significantly higher

53

specific heats than nitrogen. GateCycle™ does perform a basic chemical analysis (presuming complete combustion) to arrive at the exiting mole fractions of the exhaust constituents. This step is imperative in any combined cycle model.

Even a rudimentary combustion analysis requires knowledge of the fuel composition, though the air may be presumed standard. This is one of the reasons for fuel composition corrections to performance (i.e., power, heat rate, exhaust flow, and exhaust temperature), as the expanding products of combustion and excess air behave differently, depending on the mole fractions. I have encountered two instances where the HRSG manufacturer either presumed or was given preliminary compositions, which were sufficiently different from the final that there was insufficient energy leaving the gas turbine and entering the HRSG to produce the guaranteed steam flow—even if no heat were lost and the stack temperature were reduced to ambient—neither of these conditions being thermodynamically possible. The result was failure and a costly lawsuit.

Chapter 13. Evaporative Coolers

Evaporative coolers are just that... While their designs vary somewhat, their purpose is the same: saturate the incoming air with moisture. The performance of an evaporative cooler is called, *effectiveness*. This value varies from 75% to 95%, with a typical value of 85%. This means the air temperature leaving the evaporative cooler and entering the gas turbine is expected to be at 85% of the difference from the ambient dry-bulb temperature to the ambient wet-bulb temperature. Put another way, the device is expected to achieve 85% of the wet-bulb temperature. The calculation couldn't be simpler:

$$Tdb2 = Tdb1 + \varepsilon\left(Twb - Tdb1\right) \qquad (13.1)$$

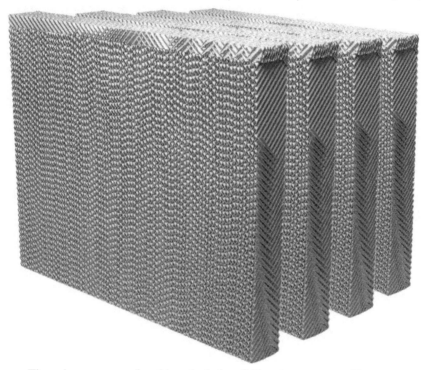

There is no excuse for this calculation failing to converge. There are no iterations involved. It's a one-and-done equation. True, you must now calculate a new value of relative humidity or moisture content, but this is a property call and not at the cycle model programming level. Property calls should never fail to return a value, any more than sin() or cos(). As this is presumed to be an adiabatic saturation process (i.e., no heat transfer) and the wet-bulb is indicative of the enthalpy, this remains constant. Furthermore, we can represent the specific enthalpy (per unit mass of dry air):

$$h = CpTdb + wHg \qquad (13.2)$$

where Cp is the specific heat of dry air, w is the humidity ratio (mass of water vapor per mass of dry air) and Hg is the enthalpy of water vapor.[16] Using the psychrometric formulation of Hyland and Wexler, as found in the 1977 ASHRAE Handbook of Fundamentals, we can write:

$$h = 0.2405Tdb + w(0.4197\text{Tdb} + 1060) \qquad (13.3)$$

Because this is an adiabatic (i.e., no heat transfer) process, the enthalpy is the same before and after. Equations 13.1 and 13.3 can be combined to yield:

$$w2 = \frac{(0.4197\,w1 + 0.2405\varepsilon)Tdb1 + 1060\,w1 - 0.2405\varepsilon Twb}{0.41967(1 - \varepsilon)Tdb1 + 0.41967\varepsilon Twb + 1060} \qquad (13.4)$$

Foggers are very similar to evaporative coolers, but aren't always effective or practical. Sometimes these are preferable when fresh water is scarce. These are handled the same computationally.

---

[16] It is often said in the literature that the last term in Equation 13.2 (i.e., the contribution of water vapor), should be the latent heat of vaporization, Hfg, but this is not true. Consider this fact… if you were to add steam at the critical point to air, you would most assuredly increase the enthalpy of the mixture, but Hfg=0 at the critical point.

Chapter 14. Chillers

Chillers are refrigeration units installed to provide colder air entering a gas turbine. As these are very expensive to purchase, maintain, and operate, they are not used as often as evaporative coolers. Chillers are even simpler to implement than evaporative coolers. Rather than being an adiabatic (i.e., no heat transfer) process, chillers are a no mass transfer process. That is, they change the enthalpy without changing the moisture content, except when condensation occurs. Thus, these are handled computationally by limiting the exit relative humidity to 100% or limiting the exit dry-bulb to the dew-point. The additional auxiliary load is most often handled by assuming a coefficient of performance (essentially the reciprocal of efficiency with units). The power consumption is then equal to the cooling load (tons[17] or kWt[18]) times the coefficient of performance (kWe/ton or kWe/kWt).

---

[17] One US cooling ton is equal to 12,000 BTU/hr, originally derived from the heat absorbed by one ton of ice melting over a 24-hour period.

[18] Kilowatts (and megawatts) may be electric (kWe) or thermal (kWt).

Chapter 15. Economizers

In the context of Heat Recovery Steam Generators (HRSGs) as part of gas turbine combined cycle power systems, economizers heat up, but do not boil, water. These are located near the exit of the HRSG relative to the gas turbine exhaust gas and the inlet of the HRSG relative to the feedwater. There may be one or more of these, depending on the number of pressures provided by the HRSG and the stages of heating. The size and placement of these components is an art as well as a science. Successful HRSG manufacturers go to great lengths to scale and position these important components, as they are expensive and the performance greatly depends on their proper function.

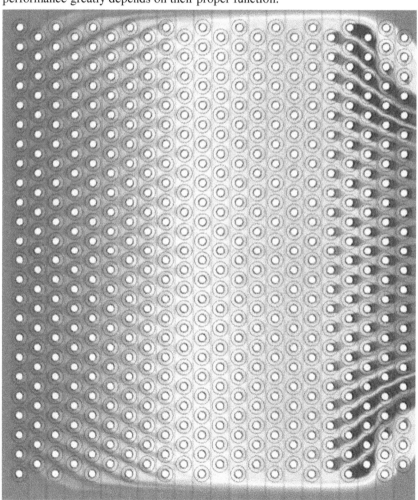

The calculations are quite simple. Since evaporation is not allowed, there is no phase change on either hot or cold side. Furthermore, there is little change in specific heat of either the exhaust gas or water in these devices. While the orientation and number of tube passes might be of considerable interest to a manufacturers, these details are of little interest in cycle modeling. There is precious little difference whether you use the NTU-effectiveness or LMTD method to analyze the heat transfer in one of these economizers. If you do not work for a manufacturer, you will be provided with the performance; therefore, how this is achieved becomes immaterial. That it does achieve the stated performance, of course, does matter; but this isn't a computational consideration.

There are remarkably few problems with GateCycle™, but one of these few that is particularly annoying occurs with economizers. As economizers are never intended to deliver steam, any software that handles them should never calculate that they do so. If you spend much time running GateCycle™ you will encounter what experienced users call the *christmas tree effect*, where the errors explode and warnings light up after an economizer delivers steam down the line to other components, such as pumps, which don't like vapor at the inlet. It's not that complicated! Simply clamp the output condition at saturated liquid and display a warning if you must, but DON'T generate any steam!

The equations governing economizers are also quite simple:

$$Q = \dot{m}_{hot}\left(h_{in} - h_{out}\right) = \dot{m}_{cold}\left(h_{out} - h_{in}\right) \tag{15.1}$$

$$Q = UA \cdot LMTD \tag{15.2}$$

Some HRSG manufacturers (e.g., Nooter-Eriksen) list either crossflow or counterflow for each of the elements. While the designation *crossflow* might be literal, it would be very hard to achieve *counterflow* in a HRSG. To do so would require horizontal steam flow in the tubes toward the gas turbine exhaust. These designations must, therefore, be taken as conceptual. GateCycle™ has quite a few options available for configuration, but these do not improve the accuracy of the final results and often cause problems.

There are two ways to implement an economizer: 1) specified water outlet temperature (or subcooling) and 2) specified UA (of course, clamped to prevent vapor). In GateCycle™ terminology, these would be *design* and *off-design* modes, respectively. Neither one of these is complicated.

61

Chapter 16. Evaporators

In the context of Heat Recovery Steam Generators (HRSGs) as part of gas turbine combined cycle power systems, evaporators accept saturated or subcooled water and deliver saturated (not superheated) steam. As there is phase change on the tube side of these heat exchangers, there is no difference between the NTU-effectiveness and LMTD methods and, in fact, GateCycle™ doesn't give you any options as to the configuration in light of this. There are two ways to implement an evaporator: 1) specified steam flow and 2) specified UA. In GateCycle™ terminology, these would be *design* and *off-design* modes, respectively.

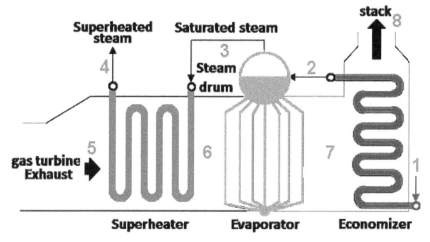

Chapter 17. Superheaters

In the context of Heat Recovery Steam Generators (HRSGs) as part of gas turbine combined cycle power systems, superheaters accept saturated vapor and deliver superheated steam. Computationally, there is precious little difference between a superheater and an economizer. The properties might be different, but the calculations are the same. There are two ways to implement a superheater: 1) specified steam outlet temperature (or degrees of superheat) and 2) specified UA. In GateCycle™ terminology, these would be *design* and *off-design* modes, respectively. The figure below shows typical superheater tubes.

Chapter 18. Solving Combined Cycle Systems

Assembling these components and solving a combined cycle can be a little tricky and convergence may be elusive, but it's not as complicated as you might have heard. Besides steam properties and the components already covered, you will need exhaust gas properties (see Appendix D).

In our first example Excel® spreadsheet solving a single-pressure, three-element HRSG, we will simply use constant specific heats. Variable specific heats is a minor addition. You will find this spreadsheet (HRSG1.xls) in the folder examples\HRSG. Refer to the picture in Chapter 16. There are only two flows and eight temperatures. The gas turbine exhaust flow and temperature are inputs, leaving the steam flow to be found iteratively.

Even if the ambient conditions and fuel composition changed, this would *not require iterative calculations*, because the correction curve methodology described in Chapter 12 is one-and-done. The combustion calculations that yield exhaust gas mole fractions is also one step and not iterative.

	A	B	C	D	E	F	G	H	I
1	GT exhaust		kJ/kg/°C	MW	point	flow	pres.	temp.	enthalpy
2	74.6%	N2	1.040	28	#	kg/s	kPa	°C	kJ/kg
3	12.4%	O2	0.919	32	1	371	9000	20.0	92.4
4	3.8%	CO2	0.844	44	2	371	8250	292.2	1301.0
5	8.3%	H2O	1.930	18	3	371	8250	297.2	2754.8
6	0.9%	Ar	0.520	40	4	371	8000	547.2	3514.9
7	100.0%	total			5	4000	2.13	600.0	631.1
8	600	°C	temp.		6	4000	2.13	532.9	560.5
9	4000	kg/s	flow		7	4000	2.13	404.6	425.6
10	1.052	kJ/kg/°C	mass wtd Cp		8	4000	2.13	298.0	313.4
11	feedwater in								
12	20	°C	temp.		UA	Q	LMTD		
13	steam out				2307	282,167	122.3	super.	
14	8000	kPa	pres.		3240	539,730	166.6	evap.	
15	pressure drops				2453	448,710	182.9	econ.	
16	250	kPa	superh.		8000	1,270,607	158.8	total	
17	750	kPa	econ.						
18	desired temps				push to solve				
19	250	°C	superh.						
20	5	°C	econ.						
21	8000	kW/°C	UA						
22	user inputs								
23	calculated								
24	don't change black numbers								

Solving this problem requires simply adjusting the steam flow (cell F3) so that the total calculated UA (cell E16) matches the user-specified value (cell A21). The push button macro uses a bisection search to accomplish this. Of course, bisections searches do not work for multivariate problems, such as a three-pressure HRSG. Before moving on to that example, we will implement the HRSG1.xls spreadsheet in C. You will find this code in the same folder. The code is quite simple:

```c
void Solver1()
{
int iter;
double Cpa,dTec,dTev,dTsh,Qec,Qev,Qsh;
double F1,F2,Fstm,UAec,UAev,UAsh,UAtot;
double H1,H2,H3,H4,P1,P2,P3,P4;
double T1,T2,T3,T4,T5,T6,T7,T8;
Cpa=(mf.N2*MW.N2*Cp.N2+mf.O2*MW.O2*Cp.O2
   +mf.CO2*MW.CO2*Cp.CO2+mf.H2O*MW.H2O*Cp.H2O
   +mf.Ar*MW.Ar*Cp.Ar)/(mf.N2*MW.N2+mf.O2*MW.O2
   +mf.CO2*MW.CO2+mf.H2O*MW.H2O+mf.Ar*MW.Ar);
P4=Pstm;
P3=P4+dP.sh;
P2=P3;
P1=P2+dP.ec;
T1=Tfw;
T3=Tsat(P3/1000.,year)-273.15;
T2=T3-dT.ec;
T4=T3+dT.sh;
T5=GT.T;
H1=HofTP(T1+273.15,P1/1000.,year);
H2=HofTP(T2+273.15,P2/1000.,year);
H3=Hg(T3+273.15,year);
H4=HofTP(T4+273.15,P4/1000.,year);
F1=1.;
F2=GT.F/8.;
printf("it flo  UA\n");
for(iter=0;iter<32;iter++)
  {
  Fstm=(F1+F2)/2.;
  Qec=Fstm*(H2-H1);
  Qev=Fstm*(H3-H2);
  Qsh=Fstm*(H4-H3);
  T6=T5-Qsh/GT.F/Cpa;
  T7=T6-Qev/GT.F/Cpa;
  T8=T7-Qec/GT.F/Cpa;
  dTsh=LMTD(T5-T4,T6-T3);
  dTev=LMTD(T6-T3,T7-T2);
  dTec=LMTD(T7-T2,T8-T1);
  UAsh=Qsh/dTsh;
  UAev=Qev/dTev;
  UAec=Qec/dTec;
  UAtot=UAsh+UAev+UAec;
  printf("%2i %3.0lf %4.0lf\n",iter,Fstm,UAtot);
  if(UAtot<UAtarget)
```

68

```
        F1=Fstm;
      else
        F2=Fstm;
      }
   }
```

The output is:

```
it  flo  UA
 0  251  4322
 1  375  8161
 2  313  5988
 3  344  6993
 4  360  7554
 5  367  7851
 6  371  8004
 7  369  7927
 8  370  7966
 9  371  7985
10  371  7994
11  371  7999
12  371  8002
13  371  8001
14  371  8000
```

The bisection converges to 4 significant figures in 14 iterations.

Iterative Solution

We began with the bisection search algorithm because it's stable and always ends after a fixed number of iterations with a reasonable solution—a very strong reason for using this algorithm. The bisection search is not practical or effective for multivariate problems, such as a three-pressure HRSG. Discussion has recently arisen regarding the use of **nonlinear constrained minimization** techniques to solve thermodynamic cycles and combined cycle systems in particular. The discussion has in part motivated this author to publish the current book. Such methods are **completely unnecessary** and quite burdensome to implement in this context.

While gas turbine combined cycle systems are fairly new compared to conventional Rankine cycle systems, the calculations are by no means novel. Just because there's a function in MatLab® or Python® and just because this procedure readily yields solutions to simple nonlinear problems, does not mean that this is an effective way to handle complex cycles. If for no other reason, you cannot generalize such cycles within MatLab® or Python® and would have to manually compose each different system in order to handle its unique peculiarities.

At least one developer has attempted to write a program that creates the script to be run in MatLab® or Python®. Why not just solve the problem and eliminate MatLab® and Python® from the process, as these provide no benefit besides enhanced debugging and error messages (unallocated arrays, uninitialized variables, array overruns, divides by zero, etc.), which the experienced software developer should be able to handle without assistance.

Before we explore algorithms that are effective, let us consider the equations we seek to solve. In seeking a target UA, we must calculate some Q/LMTD. Some choices of steam flow lead to negative temperature differences, which are thermodynamically impossible as well as a divide by zero or indeterminate logarithm. This condition is clamped in the VBA macro within the spreadsheet and HRSG1.c source code. There is a second button in the spreadsheet that generates a graph of UA vs. steam flow:

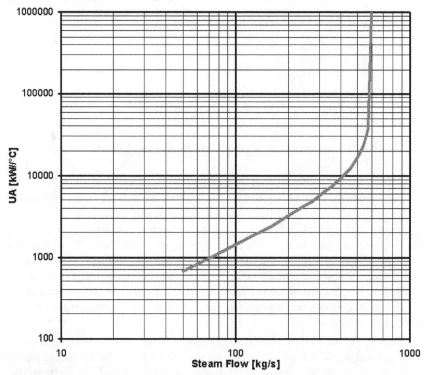

The lower left part of this curve is approximately straight, corresponding to the following relationship:

$$UA \propto flow^{\frac{4}{3}} \qquad (18.1)$$

As the flow increases to the right, we see an asymptote at flow=600 kg/s. Given this behavior, we can't use successive substitution (i.e., simple iterative replacement), as with the Rankine cycle. Furthermore, with more complex systems (e.g., a three-pressure HRSG), the asymptotes shift when the other variables change. We can easily detect and avoid these moving asymptotes. They occur when the temperature differences cross over, resulting in a zero or undefined LMTD. Instead of preventing the zero (or undefined) return value, we can utilize this information to control the iterations. With the following slight modifications to the iteration in preceding code:

```
for(iter=0;iter<32;iter++)
{
Qec=Fstm*(H2-H1);
Qev=Fstm*(H3-H2);
Qsh=Fstm*(H4-H3);
if(Qec*Qev*Qsh<=0.)
{
Fstm/=2.;
continue;
}
T6=T5-Qsh/GT.F/Cpa;
T7=T6-Qev/GT.F/Cpa;
T8=T7-Qec/GT.F/Cpa;
dTsh=LMTD2(T5-T4,T6-T3);
dTev=LMTD2(T6-T3,T7-T2);
dTec=LMTD2(T7-T2,T8-T1);
if(dTsh*dTev*dTec<=0.)
{
Fstm/=2.;
continue;
}
UAsh=Qsh/dTsh;
UAev=Qev/dTev;
UAec=Qec/dTec;
UAtotal=UAsh+UAev+UAec;
printf("%2i %3.0lf %4.0lf\n",iter,Fstm,UAtotal);
if(fabs(UAtotal/UAtarget-1.)<0.0001)
break;
Fstm*=(1.+UAtarget/UAtotal)/2.;
}
```

we achieve very rapid convergence to the solution (5 iterations):

```
it  flo  UA
 0   50  676
 1  321  6236
 2  366  7809
 3  371  7984
 4  371  7999
 5  371  8000
```

Once again, this solution didn't require advanced algorithms—just common sense and a little experience. I've been solving these same equations since 1975, when I began work on my master's thesis, *Theoretical Analysis of Heat*

71

Exchangers in an Ocean Thermal Energy Conversion System. All I had to work with at the time was FORTRAN, punch cards, and a UNIVAC mainframe. I have also provided GateCycle™ models to go with each of the examples in this chapter. The single-pressure example is:

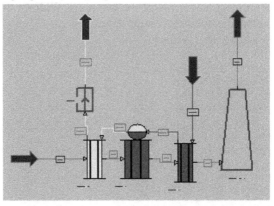

Heat Release Diagram

We will not consider the heat release diagram or a graph of temperature vs. heat transfer from the exhaust stream.

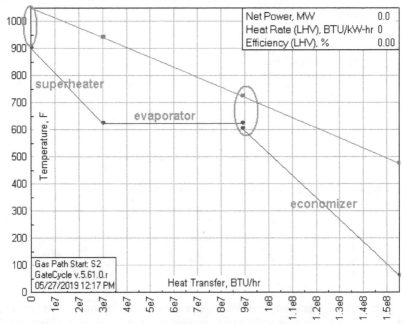

Each of the components is identified on the preceding figure. The red line is the exhaust gas, continuous and downwardly sloping, as the temperature drops over the length of the HRSG. The blue line is the steam. The economizer portion (on the right) is sloped upward, indicating rising temperature. The evaporator portion (in the middle) is horizontal, as vaporization occurs at constant temperature. The superheater portion (on the left) is also upwardly sloping, indicating rising temperature. The two potential *pinch points* are each indicated by a magenta ellipse—on the left at the exit of the superheater and in the middle at the exit of the economizer. Pinch points dominate the design and operation of HRSGs. Pinch points are what cause the asymptote in the preceding UA vs. steam flow graph.

Two-Pressure HRSG

We will now consider a two-pressure HRSG, which is considerably more complicated in the heat transfer and computations.

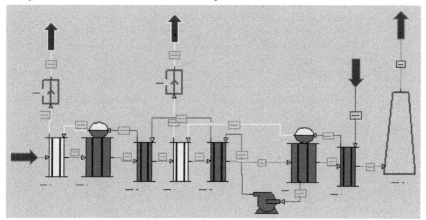

The solution procedure is similar to the single-pressure case:

```
for(iter=0;iter<32;iter++)
   {
   Qec1=(Flp+Fhp)*(Hec1-Hfw );
   Qev1= Flp     *(Hev1-Hec1);
   Qsh1= Flp     *(Hsh1-Hev1);
   Qec2= Fhp     *(Hec2-Hbfw);
   Qec3= Fhp     *(Hec3-Hec2);
   Qev2= Fhp     *(Hev2-Hec3);
   Qsh2= Fhp     *(Hsh2-Hev2);
   if(Qec1<=0.||Qev1<=0.||Qsh1<=0.||Qec2<=0.
   ||Qec3<=0.||Qev2<=0.||Qsh2<=0.)
      {
      Flp/=2.;
      Fhp/=2.;
```

```c
      continue;
      }
T1=GT.T;
T2=T1-Qsh2/GT.F/Cp;
T3=T2-Qev2/GT.F/Cp;
T4=T3-Qec3/GT.F/Cp;
T5=T4-Qsh1/GT.F/Cp;
T6=T5-Qec2/GT.F/Cp;
T7=T6-Qev1/GT.F/Cp;
T8=T7-Qec1/GT.F/Cp;
dTsh2=LMTD(T1-Tsh2,T2-Tev2);
dTev2=LMTD(T2-Tev2,T3-Tec3);
dTec3=LMTD(T3-Tec3,T4-Tec2);
dTsh1=LMTD(T4-Tsh1,T5-Tev1);
dTec2=LMTD(T5-Tec2,T6-Tbfw);
dTev1=LMTD(T6-Tev1,T7-Tec1);
dTec1=LMTD(T7-Tec1,T8-Tfw );
if(dTsh2<=0.||dTev2<=0.||dTec3<=0.||dTec2<=0.
||dTsh1<=0.||dTev1<=0.||dTec1<=0.)
      {
      Flp/=2.;
      Fhp/=2.;
      continue;
      }
UAhp=Qsh2/dTsh2+Qev2/dTev2+Qec3/dTec3+Qec2/dTec2;
UAlp=Qsh1/dTsh1+Qev1/dTev1+Qec1/dTec1;
printf("%2i %5.0lf %6.0lf %6.0lf
%6.0lf\n",iter,Flp,Fhp,UAlp,UAhp);
if(fabs(UAlp/UAtarget.LP-1.)<0.0001)
   if(fabs(UAhp/UAtarget.HP-1.)<0.0001)
      break;
Flp*=(1.+UAtarget.LP/UAlp)/2.;
Fhp*=(1.+UAtarget.HP/UAhp)/2.;
}
```

The same simple iteration scheme converges quickly:

```
it  Flp    Fhp     UAlp    UAhp
 0 10000   50000   47791  170617
 1 25925  112916  349238  706947
 2 20385  104375  220166  572877
 3 19452  106846  225399  606762
 4 18356  106251  212056  598037
 5 17834  106425  208317  600381
 6 17478  106391  204998  599823
 7 17265  106407  203210  599997
 8 17129  106407  202022  599970
```

A generalized program handling a variety of configurations would require a more complex algorithm, which we will consider in the next section, as we increase to a three-pressure HRSG. The heat release diagram for this system has

74

four potential pinch points. The blue lines are the LP steam path and the green lines are the HP steam path. There is a horizontal (flat) section for each evaporator.

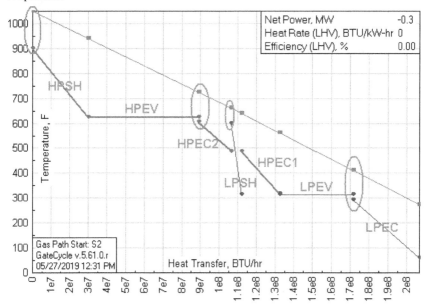

Notice that the HP economizer is split into two sections and the LP superheater is inserted between the two. If this were not so, the blue LPSH line would be shifted right, intersecting the downward-sloping gas temperature curve, resulting in a pinch and limiting the available degrees of superheat. This is why manufacturers create so many sections and position them strategically along the gas path.

Three-Pressure HRSG without Reheat

This is the simplest type of three-pressure HRSG and is more of a computational example than a practical design. In practice, there will almost always be reheat with a three-pressure HRSG. We begin with almost the same code as the two-pressure HRSG, only we construct it so that the HP, IP, and LP evaporator flow rates are inputs and the UAs are the outputs. This organization easily lends itself to nonlinear equation solvers so that we can consider which are more or less effective. With each of these examples, we are moving closer to a generalized solution, so note the changes in source code that facilitate this progression. In this third program (HRSG3.c), we also implement variable specific heats for the gas stream. The system is shown in the following figure:

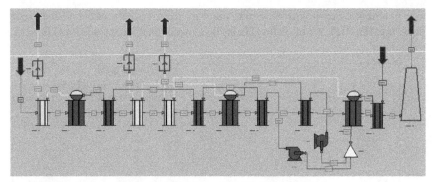

The heat release diagram for this system is shown below:

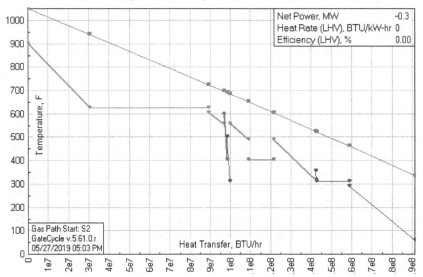

The LP steam path is blue, the IP is green, and the HP is magenta. There are three horizontal sections plus more potential pinch points. The inner loop that calculates the critical parameters is:

```
void Loop(double Flp,double Fip,double Fhp)
    {
    printf(" %5.0lf %5.0lf %6.0lf",Flp,Fip,Fhp);

/* heat transfer for each element */

    Qlpec=(Flp+Fip+Fhp)*(lpec.H-lpfw.H);
    Qlpev=Flp*(lpev.H-lpec.H)        /* lp steam */
         +(Fip+Fhp)*(Hlf-lpec.H); /* sat lqd */
    Qlpsh=Flp*(lpsh.H-lpev.H);
    Qipec=Fip*(ipec.H-ipfw.H);
```

76

```c
Qipev=Fip*(ipev.H-ipec.H);
Qipsh=Fip*(ipsh.H-ipev.H);
Qhpe1=Fhp*(hpe1.H-hpfw.H);
Qhpe2=Fhp*(hpe2.H-hpe1.H);
Qhpe3=Fhp*(hpe3.H-hpe2.H);
Qhpev=Fhp*(hpev.H-hpe3.H);
Qhpsh=Fhp*(hpsh.H-hpev.H);
if(Qlpec<=0.||Qlpev<=0.||Qlpsh<=0.||Qipec<=0.
  ||Qipev<=0.||Qipsh<=0.||Qhpe1<=0.||Qhpe2<=0.
  ||Qhpe3<=0.||Qhpev<=0.||Qhpsh<=0.)
  {
  UAhp=UAip=UAlp=0.;
  printf(" %6.0lf %6.0lf %6.0lf\n",UAlp,UAip,UAhp);
  return;
  }

/* gas path enthalpies */

H01=Hgas(GT.T);
H02=H01-Qhpsh/GT.F;
H03=H02-Qhpev/GT.F;
H04=H03-Qhpe3/GT.F;
H05=H04-Qipsh/GT.F;
H06=H05-Qlpsh/GT.F;
H07=H06-Qhpe2/GT.F;
H08=H07-Qipev/GT.F;
H09=H08-Qhpe1/GT.F;
H10=H09-Qipec/GT.F;
H11=H10-Qlpev/GT.F;
H12=H11-Qipec/GT.F;

/* gas path temperatures */

T01=GT.T;
T02=Tgas(H02);
T03=Tgas(H03);
T04=Tgas(H04);
T05=Tgas(H05);
T06=Tgas(H06);
T07=Tgas(H07);
T08=Tgas(H08);
T09=Tgas(H09);
T10=Tgas(H10);
T11=Tgas(H11);
T12=Tgas(H12);

/* temperature differences */

dThpsh=LMTD(T01-hpsh.T,T02-hpev.T);
```

77

```
dThpev=LMTD(T02-hpev.T,T03-hpe3.T);
dThpe3=LMTD(T03-hpe3.T,T04-ipsh.T);
dTipsh=LMTD(T04-ipsh.T,T05-lpsh.T);
dTlpsh=LMTD(T05-lpsh.T,T06-hpe2.T);
dThpe2=LMTD(T06-hpe2.T,T07-ipev.T);
dTipev=LMTD(T07-ipev.T,T08-hpe1.T);
dThpe1=LMTD(T08-hpe1.T,T09-ipec.T);
dTipec=LMTD(T09-ipec.T,T10-lpev.T);
dTlpev=LMTD(T10-lpev.T,T11-lpec.T);
dTlpec=LMTD(T11-lpec.T,T12-lpfw.T);
if(dTlpec<=0.||dTlpev<=0.||dTlpsh<=0.||
   dTipec<=0.||dTipev<=0.||dTipsh<=0.||
   dThpe1<=0.||dThpe2<=0.||dThpe3<=0.||
   dThpev<=0.||dThpsh<=0.)
{
UAhp=UAip=UAlp=0.;
printf(" %6.0lf %6.0lf %6.0lf\n",UAlp,UAip,UAhp);
return;
}

/* conductances */

UAhpsh=Qhpsh/dThpsh;
UAhpev=Qhpev/dThpev;
UAhpe3=Qhpe3/dThpe3;
UAipsh=Qipsh/dTipsh;
UAlpsh=Qlpsh/dTlpsh;
UAhpe2=Qhpe2/dThpe2;
UAipev=Qipev/dTipev;
UAhpe1=Qhpe1/dThpe1;
UAipec=Qipec/dTipec;
UAlpev=Qlpev/dTlpev;
UAlpec=Qlpec/dTlpec;

UAhp=UAhpe1+UAhpe2+UAhpe3+UAhpev+UAhpsh;
UAip=UAipec+UAipev+UAipsh;
UAlp=UAlpec+UAlpev+UAlpsh;
printf(" %6.0lf %6.0lf %6.0lf\n",UAlp,UAip,UAhp);
}
```

This also converges quickly using the same simplistic correction:

```
it  Flp    Fip    Fhp    UAlp    UAip   UAhp
 0  5000   5000   50000  35585   12734  176895
 1  16551  12317  95664  167234  58189  494465
 2  18172  11450  96199  177425  54252  499263
 3  19329  11001  96270  184250  52042  499556
 4  20155  10785  96313  189527  51008  499847
 5  20712  10679  96327  193207  50502  499950
 6  21076  10626  96332  195674  50254  499991
 7  21309  10599  96333  197278  50130  500004
```

Convergence

At this point the reader might be concerned that such a simplistic algorithm would often fail to converge and that these examples only converge because the starting values were carefully selected. This is not the case. In fact, I have set up HRSG3.c for random initial values and to run endlessly demonstrating convergence. Consider the following code snippet from the program:

```
if(use_random_initial_values)
    {
    Flp=100*randbetween(1,10000);
    Fip=100*randbetween(1,10000);
    Fhp=100*randbetween(1,10000);
    }
else
    {
    Flp=GT.F/200.;
    Fip=GT.F/200.;
    Fhp=GT.F/ 20.;
    }
```

Even in the first example (HRSG1.c), we backed off the asymptote, dividing the flow by 2. In that example we used a simple one-half damping. A slightly more sophisticated damping is quite effective:

```
damp=1.;
for(i=iter=0;iter<128;iter++)
    {
    d=1.+1./damp;
    printf("%2i %6.4lf",iter,damp);
    Loop(Flp,Fip,Fhp);
    if(UAlp<=0.||UAip<=0.||UAhp<=0.)
        {
        Flp/=2.;
        Fip/=2.;
        Fhp/=2.;
        if(i)
            damp+=2.;
        continue;
        }
    if(fabs(UAlp/UAtarget.lp-1.)<0.0001)
        if(fabs(UAip/UAtarget.ip-1.)<0.0001)
            if(fabs(UAhp/UAtarget.hp-1.)<0.0001)
                return(1);
    i++;
    d=1.+1./damp;
    Flp=fmax(Flp/d,fmin(Flp*d,
    Flp*(1.+UAtarget.lp/UAlp)/2.));
    Fip=fmax(Fip/d,fmin(Fip*d,
    Fip*(1.+UAtarget.ip/UAip)/2.));
```

79

```
Fhp=fmax(Fhp/d,fmin(Fhp*d,
Fhp*(1.+UAtarget.hp/UAhp)/2.));
    }
```

This scheme was allowed to run through thousands of cases, each having different random initial values. None failed to converge.

Reheat & Duct Burner

The only remaining modifications needed to complete the typical HRSG design is reheat steam and a duct burner. The associated files are named HRSG4 in the same folder. Although arrangements vary with application and manufacturer, the following is typical:

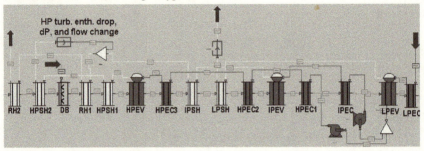

The heat release diagram:

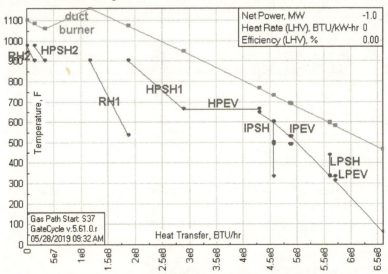

Variants include: two or three HP and/or RH superheaters, the order of the final two superheaters (HP or RH), and the order and number of HP economizers. Some HRSG manufacturers split the gas flow and put two components in parallel at the same position along the gas path. All of these variations are intended to minimize pinch points and reduce the required surface area and cost of materials. Notice the very small IP and LP steam produced with duct firing. This is typical. The stack temperature may also be lower with duct firing than without. While this may seem counterintuitive, upon closer examination, it is not. As I mentioned previously, HRSGs are controlled by pinch points. The upward shift in the gas line changes the location of the pinch points in fired cases, often greatly diminishing the LP steam production. Some heat balances even show this as zero, though the LP evaporator still serves as a deaerator, so some minute steam flow is necessary. Some arrangements may appear odd at first, but such peculiarities are often intentional to facilitate stable operation with and without duct firing.

In this example, the cold reheat steam (CRH) is calculated from the main steam by simple flow and pressure ratios and a constant enthalpy drop. In a complete system, this would be accounted for when solving the steam turbine. Note also that the gas mole fractions change downstream of the duct burner. We will discuss chemistry and gas mole fractions in Appendix D. The CRH must be mixed with the IP steam to determine the RH1 inlet conditions. As this depends on the HP/IP steam flow ratio, this calculation must be moved inside the flow iteration loop. The same algorithm is used, which converges adequately:

it	Flp	Fip	Fhp	UAlp	UAip	UAhp
0	15000	15000	150000	99769	31738	590832
1	30000	19316	265409	291330	66992	1402578
2	40744	16866	274627	356163	61323	1491831
3	48971	15309	275379	394473	55787	1496200
4	55522	14515	275729	426445	52994	1498420
5	60310	14105	275874	450598	51565	1499398
6	63616	13891	275929	467671	50828	1499807
7	65815	13778	275947	479212	50444	1499967
8	67242	13717	275950	486786	50241	1500020
9	68155	13684	275948	491664	50132	1500032
10	68733	13666	275945	494767	50074	1500029
11	69096	13656	275943	496725	50042	1500022
12	69324	13650	275941	497954	50024	1500016

Single-Pressure Combined Cycle Power Plant

By combining the GT corrections in Chapter 12 plus sections of code from cycle1.c and HRSG1.c, we can construct a single-pressure combined cycle power plant model (CCPP1.c). You will find the files in folder examples\CCPP. This is the simplest combined cycle arrangement and we will keep the details to a minimum. We will consider additional details in the next section. If you are able to run the GateCycle™ model provided, you will notice that the steam turbine will always generate errors. This is unavoidable due to the implicit implementation of the SCC method, whether it's necessary or not given the current configuration. The system is shown in this next figure:

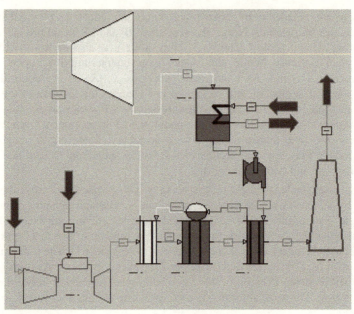

The heat release diagram is shown in this next figure:

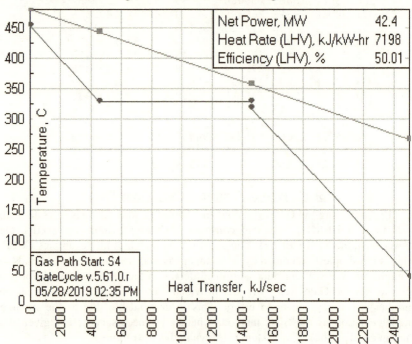

The entire solution code is brief and straightforward:

```
void CCPP(double baro,double Tamb,double RH,double Tccw)
  {
  int iter;
  double dTec,dTev,dTsh,Fstm,Qec,Qev,Qfu,Qsh,T1,
    T2,T3,T4,UAec,UAev,UAsh,UAto;
  GT gt;
  TPH bfw,cnd,eco,evp,mst,uep;
  struct{double cnd,net,pmp,stg;}kW;
  gt=GasTurbinePerformance(baro,Tamb,RH);
  Qfu=gt.kWnet*gt.kJkWh/3600.;
  mst.T=Tstm;
  Fstm=gt.EGW/50.;
  uep.T=Tccw+10.;
  printf("it Fstm Tcond UAtot\n");
  for(iter=0;iter<32;iter++)
    {
    mst.P=stg.swc*Fstm;
    mst.H=HofTP(mst.T,mst.P,year);
    uep.P=Psat(uep.T,year);
    Turbine(mst.P,mst.H,uep.P,stg.eff,&uep.H);
    kW.stg=Fstm*(mst.H-uep.H);
    cnd.T=Tsat(uep.P,year);
    cnd.H=Hf(cnd.T,year);
    kW.cnd=Fstm*(uep.H-cnd.H);
    cnd.T=Tcond(kW.cnd,Tccw);
    cnd.P=Psat(cnd.T,year);
    evp.P=mst.P+0.2;
    evp.T=Tsat(evp.P,year);
    evp.H=Hg(evp.T,year);
    eco.P=evp.P;
    eco.T=evp.T-5.;
    eco.H=HofTP(eco.T,eco.P,year);
    bfw.P=evp.P+0.8;
    Pump(cnd.P,cnd.H,bfw.P,bfp.eff,&bfw.H);
    kW.pmp=Fstm*(bfw.H-cnd.H);
    kW.net=gt.kWnet+kW.stg*gen.eff-kW.pmp;
    Qsh=Fstm*(mst.H-evp.H);
    Qev=Fstm*(evp.H-eco.H);
    Qec=Fstm*(eco.H-bfw.H);
    if(Qsh<=0.||Qev<=0.||Qec<=0.)
      {
      Fstm/=2.;
      continue;
      }
    T1=gt.EGT;
    T2=T1-Qsh/gt.EGW/Cp;
    T3=T2-Qev/gt.EGW/Cp;
    T4=T3-Qec/gt.EGW/Cp;
```

```
        dTsh=LMTD(T1-mst.T,T2-evp.T);
        dTev=LMTD(T2-evp.T,T3-eco.T);
        dTec=LMTD(T3-eco.T,T4-bfw.T);
        if(dTsh<=0.||dTev<=0.||dTec<=0.)
          {
          Fstm/=2.;
          continue;
          }
        UAec=Qec/dTec;
        UAev=Qev/dTev;
        UAsh=Qsh/dTsh;
        UAto=UAec+UAev+UAsh;
        printf("%2i %4.2lf %5.1lf
    %5.1lf\n",iter,Fstm,cnd.T,UAto);
        if(fabs(UAto/UAta-1.)<0.0001)
          if(fabs(uep.T-cnd.T)<0.5)
            break;
        Fstm=fmax(Fstm/1.5,fmin(Fstm*1.5,
            Fstm*(UAta/UAto+1.)/2.));
        uep.T=(uep.T+cnd.T)/2.;
        }
      printf("kWnet=%.0lf, kJ/kWh=%.0lf\n",kW.net,
        Qfu*3600./kW.net);
      }
```

The iterations quickly converge, even with the simplest algorithm:

```
it Fstm Tcond UAtot
 0 5.93 301.5 159.2
 1 6.68 302.8 195.7
 2 6.76 302.9 199.2
 3 6.77 302.9 199.7
 4 6.78 302.9 199.9
 5 6.78 302.9 199.9
 6 6.78 302.9 200.0
 7 6.78 303.0 200.0
kWnet=52771, kJ/kWh=7657
```

Triple-Pressure Combined Cycle Power Plant

By adding sections of code from HRSG4.c, we can construct a triple-pressure combined cycle power plant model (CCPP4.c). You will find the files in folder examples\CCPP. We see in the following code snippet that the pumps and steam turbine sections have been brought inside the iteration loop, as the changing flows impact the operation of these components. The flow through each steam turbine section determines the pressures in the HRSG, which impacts the amount of steam produced. The same pump and turbine functions from cycle1.c are used here, as they are the same, regardless of whether this is a conventional or combined cycle system.

84

```
/* IP steam path properties */

    ipsh.P=rh0.P;
    ipev.P=ipsh.P+dPsh.ip;
    ipec.P=ipev.P;
    ipfw.P=ipec.P+dPec.ip;
    ipev.T=Tsat(ipev.P,year);
    ipec.T=ipev.T-dTec.ip;
    Pump(lpev.P,Hlf,ipec.P,ipp.eff,&ipfw.H);
    ipfw.T=TofPH(ipec.P,ipfw.H,year);
    ipsh.T=Tsh.ip;
    ipfw.H=HofTP(ipfw.T,ipfw.P,year);
    ipec.H=HofTP(ipec.T,ipec.P,year);
    ipev.H=Hg(ipev.T,year);
    ipsh.H=HofTP(ipsh.T,ipsh.P,year);

/* mix CRH and IP steam and update T,H */

    crh.P=rh0.P;
    Turbine(hps2.P,hps2.H,crh.P,hpt.eff,&crh.H);
    rh0.H=(Frh*crh.H+Fip*ipsh.H)/(Frh+Fip);
    rh0.T=TofPH(rh0.P,rh0.H,year);

/* IPT exit/LPT inlet */

    ipt2.P=lpt1.P=lpsh.P;
    Turbine(rh2.P,rh2.H,ipt2.P,ipt.eff,&ipt2.H);
    lpt1.H=(Frh*ipt2.H+Flp*lpsh.H)/(Frh+Flp);
    lpt2.P=Psat(Tcnd,year);
    Turbine(lpt1.P,lpt1.H,lpt2.P,lpt.eff,&lpt2.H);
    Qcnd=(Frh+Flp)*(lpt2.H-cnd.H);
```

The system is shown in this next figure:

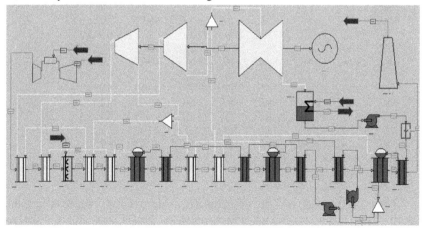

85

The heat release diagram is very similar to the previous three-pressure:

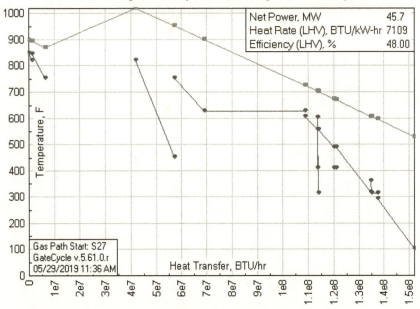

Net Power, MW	45.7
Heat Rate (LHV), BTU/kW-hr	7109
Efficiency (LHV), %	48.00

Gas Path Start: S27
GateCycle v.5.61.0.r
05/29/2019 11:36 AM

Heat Transfer, BTU/hr

Typical model output is listed below:

```
three-pressure combined cycle power plant model
ambient: 0.7726,0.2073,0.0004,0.0092,0.0106
exhaust: 0.7726,0.1959,0.0045,0.0092,0.0178
ductbrn: 0.7726,0.1946,0.0050,0.0092,0.0187
it   Flp   Fip   Fhp  Tcn   UAlp   UAip    UAhp
 0  2000  8333  83333 100  74749  48571  686891
 1  2003  8456  84129 100  77038  50408  706775
 2  1977  8422  83725 100  75817  49649  696711
 3  1966  8452  83923 100  76313  50103  701668
 4  1949  8443  83823 100  75949  49914  699196
 5  1937  8450  83871  99  76010  50024  700408
 6  1924  8448  83847  99  75866  49978  699805
 7  1913  8450  83859  99  75831  50005  700101
 8  1903  8449  83853  99  75750  49994  699953
 9  1893  8450  83855  99  75699  50000  700026
10  1885  8450  83854  99  75641  49998  699990
11  1877  8450  83854  99  75593  49999  700007
12  1869  8450  83854  99  75546  49999  699998
GT=43273 kW, ST=6705 kW, total=49978 kW
Heat Rate=7998 BTU/kWh
fuel: GT=18294, DB=2205
```

Note the three air/gas sets of calculated mole fractions that feed into the specific heat functions. The net power output of the GT and ST are listed, as

86

well as the sum and the net heat rate. The auxiliary power is deducted from the ST output. The fuel flows are listed at the end. The main program is set up to create correction curves for the combined cycle. Abbreviated output is listed below:

```
baro,kW,BTU/kWh
13.696,46903,8523
14.696,49978,7998
15.696,53042,7536

Tdb,kW,BTU/kWh
0,56183,7724
10,55153,7770
50,51017,7953
60,49978,7998
110,44784,8215
115,44266,8235
120,43749,8255

RH,kW,BTU/kWh
0.00,49789,7994
0.60,49978,7998
0.65,49994,7999
0.70,50010,7999
0.75,50026,7999
0.80,50041,8000
0.95,50089,8001
1.00,50105,8001
```

The results were piped to a CSV file and pulled into the Excel® spreadsheet, CCPP4.xls. The main program is organized to facilitate calculations for correction curves.

```
int main(int argc,char**argv,char**envp)
{
double baro=14.696; /* barometric pressure [psia] */
double Tdb=60.;      /* ambient temperature [F] */
double RH=0.60;      /* ambient relative humidity */
double Tccw=60.;/* cooling water inlet temp. [F] */
double Qdb=43E6;/* duct burner heat input [BTU/hr] */
printf("three-pressure combined cycle power plant
  model\n");
CCPP(baro,Tdb,RH,Tccw,Qdb,1);
for(baro=13.696;baro<15.697;baro+=0.1)
  {
  CCPP(baro,60.,0.6,Tccw,Qdb,0);
  printf("%.3lf,%.0lf,%.0lf\n",baro,kW.tot,HtRt);
  }
for(Tdb=0.;Tdb<121.;Tdb+=5.)
  {
  CCPP(14.696,Tdb,0.6,Tccw,Qdb,0);
```

```
    printf("%.0lf,%.0lf,%.0lf\n",Tdb,kW.tot,HtRt);
    }
  for(RH=0.;RH<1.01;RH+=0.05)
    {
    CCPP(14.696,60.,RH,Tccw,Qdb,0);
    printf("%.2lf,%.0lf,%.0lf\n",RH,kW.tot,HtRt);
    }
  return(0);
  }
```

The temperature correction curve is:

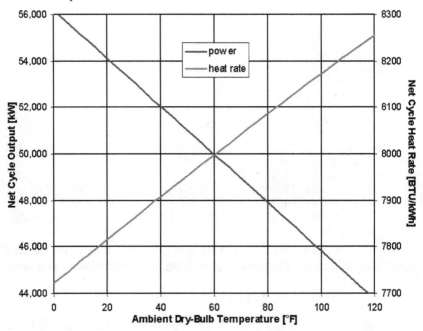

The curves are nearly straight due to the simplistic GT corrections. More detailed corrections were discussed in Chapter 12 and may be found in the LM6000 spreadsheet.

The pressure correction is expected to be straight lines:

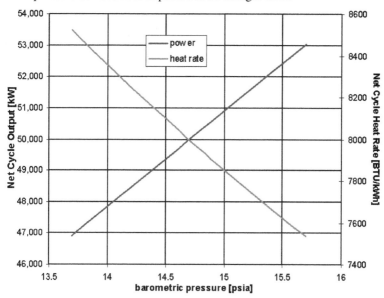

The relative humidity curve is almost flat in this case, which would not be the case with an evaporative cooler.

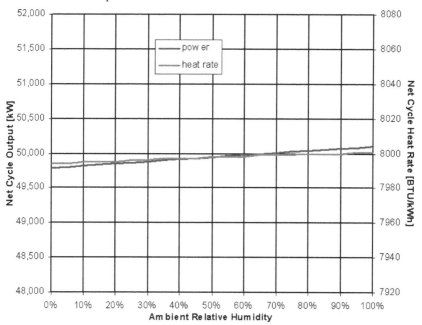

Most often, the relative humidity correction is a fan of curves at several different ambient temperatures. You could add an evaporative cooler or chiller at the inlet to create curves that account for these components. The generator losses in CCPP4.c are also rather simplistic. More sophisticated curves may be found in the examples\generator\generator.xls spreadsheet.

Chapter 19. Other Cycles

There are many more types of cycles, including: Otto, Diesel, Brayton, Lenoir, Stirling, and Ericsson. These are so simple to implement by comparison to Rankine or combined cycle systems that they will only be mentioned in passing. You will find a spreadsheet (cycles.xls) in the examples/other folder that contains each of these.

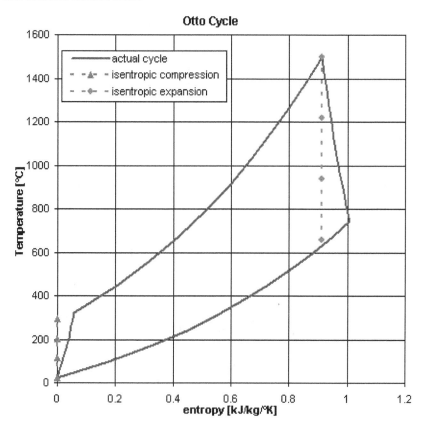

The spreadsheet includes calculations, properties, and several graphs to illustrate the processes for each cycle. You can change the conditions and efficiencies to see what impact these have on the power.

The P vs. V diagram for the Otto cycle is:

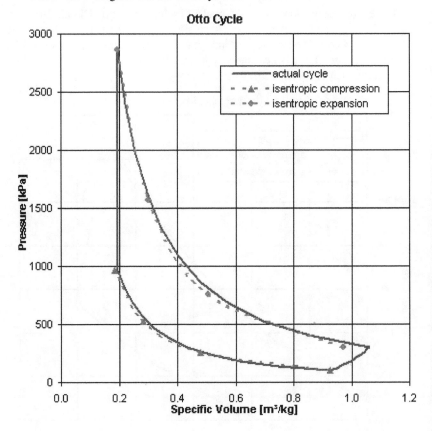

The T vs. S diagram for the Diesel cycle is:

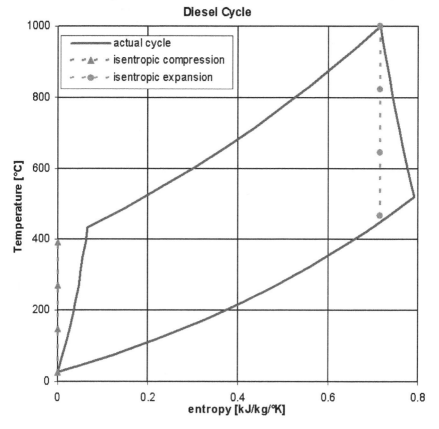

Diesel Cycle

The P vs. V diagram for the Brayton cycle is:

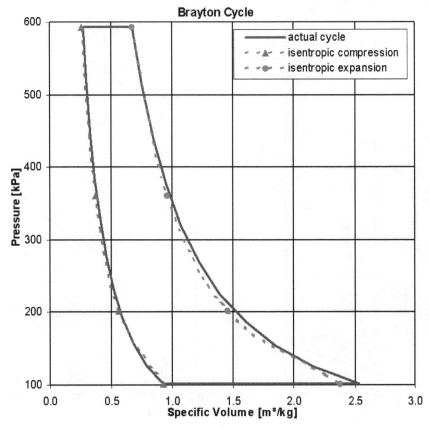

Brayton Cycle

Legend:
— actual cycle
- -▲- - isentropic compression
- -●- - isentropic expansion

X-axis: Specific Volume [m³/kg]
Y-axis: Pressure [kPa]

Appendix A. GateCycle™

GateCycle™ is a very powerful thermodynamic cycle modeling tool and remarkable software product owned by the General Electric Company (GE). It is shockingly expensive, but so are the various competing products. Sadly, GE has abandoned this proverbial goose that laid the golden egg (and ejected the original development team). Here I refer to version 5.61.0.r, not version 6 and beyond. In my opinion, the user interface accompanying version 6 is dreadful, making the whole 6th generation thing rubbish.

Though it is no longer sold, you may be able to purchase a hardlock key on E-bay, which will work with version 5.61. GateCycle™ was designed to run on Windows® XP®. It is complicated, but impossible to install on Windows® 7. When doing so, DO NOT install *anything* in either the Program Files or Program Data folders. After installation, right click on the desktop icon and set the compatibility to Windows® XP®. You will also need a version of Microsoft® Excel® no more recent than 2003, as the Add-In CycleLink™ will not work on newer versions. Before long this will no longer be possible and there are no plans to remedy the situation.

95

Appendix B: C Compilers

Everything you need to build applications written in C for the Windows® operating system can be obtained without cost. There are several compilers that you can find on the Internet. They each have different strengths and weaknesses.

The Microsoft® C Compiler

Go to www.microsoft.com or search for "SDK download." I recommend Version 7.0A or 7.1 of the Software Development Kit. You will also need Version 7.0 of the Driver Development Kit (DDK). These are both free downloads. Microsoft® Visual Studio® is an Interactive Development and Debugging Environment (IDDE) and is entirely superfluous. The C compiler, resource compiler, and linker all come with the SDK and DDK, so there's no point purchasing Visual Studio®. The DDK also includes a cross-compiler. This allows you to create 64 bit applications on a 32 bit machine. You'll find this compiler in a folder named …\bin\x86\amd64\. You can also build 32 bit applications on a 64 bit machine. You'll find that compiler in a folder named, …\bin\amd64\x86\. Keep the two compilers in separate folders.

The Digital Mars C Compiler

Walter Bright wrote the first single-pass C++ compiler. It was called Zortech®. Symantec® picked it up for several years but dumped it when they realized it wasn't profitable. Walter Bright retained the rights and you can now download this excellent compiler for free off the Internet. The Digital Mars C compiler will only create 32 bit native executables. There are no plans at this time to add 64 bit capability. You don't really need 64 bit executables except for Excel Add-Ins. If you have a 64 bit copy of MSOffice® you must also have a 64 bit compiler and linker in order to create compatible Add-Ins for it.

Walter Bright's compilers don't optimize code as tightly as the Microsoft® compiler, but it is much more reliable. For the first two decades of its existence, the Microsoft® optimizing C compiler was slow and very buggy. There have been considerable improvements in the past decade so that it is now fast and reliable.

The most amazing feature of Walter Bright's compilers is the *trace generating* functionality, which is activated with the -gt option. When this option is activated the application runs *very* slowly, but when it's done, it leaves behind a list (TRACE.LOG) of every function, how many times it was called, by what other function, and how long it took. You can use this information to optimize and structure your code.

If you run the application again without deleting this file, it will accumulate the sums. This marvelous feature that Walter Bright has built into his compilers requires no additional effort on your part. You will be surprised to discover that for most applications a few functions completely dominate the runtime.

Other C Compilers

While some of the Gnu® tools and code can be made to function on the Windows® platform, you will find this quite a hassle. Everything Gnu® is developed within an entirely different framework—hardware and mentality. It can be done, but you will waste a lot of time doing it. I have a copy of the Watcom® C compiler, but have never opened it or had adequate motivation to do so, considering Microsoft® and Digital Mars®, which more than adequately meet my needs.

The Intel® compiler was free at one time, but now costs $699. Unless you're specifically developing applications for parallel processing there's no point, especially when other compilers are available for free. The optimization features that come with the Intel® compiler are useful, but nothing can come close to Walter Bright's -gt! The similar features of the Intel® compiler are a big hassle by comparison.

Appendix C: QUEST Program

QUick Estimation of Steam Turbine performance (QUEST) can handle most conventional coal-fired and oil-fired steam power systems. It uses the Spencer, Cotton, Cannon (SCC) method mentioned previously. This method involves a great many graphs and empirical relationships, which are too complicated to explain here. I suggest you acquire a copy of the paper online. You can get the program off my web site:

https://www.dudleybenton.altervista.org/software/index.html

At the time of this writing, there is a command line version (often called a DOS program, but this is not technically correct, as it is actually a Win32 console application). There is also a rudimentary Windows version in progress. When that is complete, I will post that at the same location. QUEST comes with 41 actual plant examples. Abbreviated output is listed below:

```
reading model: BRF.QUE
English units
TVA's Bull Run Steam Plant (950 MW nominal)
* this is a QUEST configuration file
5 one HP, one IP, and one LP turbine, with reheat
* Tb Pb Fb Tr BP
1004 3515 6335200 1000 1.50
*HP turbine stages
2
*HP turbine type
2
*HP turbine generator connection
1
*HP turbine flow factor(s)
237.20
120.50
*HPT throttle leak to reheater exit/IPT inlet
6000
*HPT throttle leak to SSR
2000
*HPT HP seal leak to SSR
-3800
*HPT HP seal leak to open feedwater heater
-10700
*HPT HP seal leak to HPT exit/reheater inlet
-35500
*HPT LP seal leak to open feedwater heater
-4600
*HPT LP seal leak to SSR
-4200
*IP turbine stages
1
*IP turbine type
```

99

```
4
*IP turbine generator connection
1
*IP turbine flow factor(s)
39.46
*IPT LP seal leak to open feedwater heater
0
*IPT LP seal leak to SSR
-6400
*cross-over pressure drop factor
.00
*LP turbine stages
4
*LP turbine type
7
*LP turbine generator connection
2
*LP turbine flow factor(s)
6.514
1.987
0.910
*LPT LP seal leak to SSR
2400
*last stage annulus area in square feet (single flow)
123.8
*number of annuli
4
*FP turbine stages
3
*FP turbine type
9
*FP turbine supply (1-7: HPT, 8-14:IPT, 15-21:LPT, 91:B,
    93:R)
1
*FP turbine flow factor(s)
449.69
211.18
95.78
*generator 1 type
3 3600-rpm conductor-cooled
*generator 1 rated KVA
475000
*generator 2 type
4 1800-rpm conductor-cooled
*generator 2 rated KVA
475000
*makeup flow
0
*makeup injection
```

```
H=hotwell
*boiler pressure drop and efficiency
15.0 90.5
*reheater pressure drop and efficiency
10.0 90.5
*number of heat exchangers
9
*heat exchanger type, TTD, DCA, shell pressure drop
* type 1: no drain inlet, type 2: drain inlet, type 3:
  open
*type TTD DCA DP
1 .0 10.0 8.1
2 5.0 10.0 5.0
2 5.0 10.0 6.9
2 5.0 10.0 7.1
3 .0 .0 7.0
1 5.0 10.0 7.9
2 5.0 10.0 8.0
2 5.0 10.0 7.8
YES, last heat exchanger before GSC drains to condenser
*boiler feedpump efficiency
85.0
*SSR flow to GSC
4400
*SSR flow to condenser
0
*SSR flow to LP turbine seals
4800
*service load (+KW or -%)
-2.50
file=C:\Development\Thermodynamics\QUEST\BRF.QUE,
  error=0
```

QUEST/2.10: QUick Estimation of Steam Turbine Power
    Cycle Performance
by Dudley J. Benton, Knoxville, Tennessee,
    dudley.benton@gmail.com

Turbine and generator performance is from "A Method for
    Predicting the
Performance of Steam Turbine-Generators... 16,500 kW and
    Larger," by R.C.
Spencer, K.C. Cotton, and C.N. Cannon, General Electric,
    1974 and ASME
paper No. 62-WA-209, 1962.

Steam properties are 1967 in accordance with standard
    G.E. practice.

```
05/24/2019 13:08
title: TVA's Bull Run Steam Plant (950 MW nominal)

Tb = 1004.0 boiler exit temperature (F)
Pb = 3515.0 boiler exit pressure (psia)
TFR= 1.0000 throttle flow ratio
Fb = 6335200 boiler flow (lb/hr)
Tr = 1000.0 reheat temperature (F)
CR = 10.000 reheater pressure drop (%)
BP = 1.500 backpressure (inches Hg)
initializing flows
adjusting flows
adjusting flows
adjusting flows
adjusting extractions
HEX 1 extraction 316760 -> 483070
HEX 2 extraction 316760 -> 477655
HEX 3 extraction 211173 -> 300658
HEX 4 extraction 316760 -> 266553
HEX 5 extraction 211173 -> 221737
HEX 6 extraction 316760 -> 309705
HEX 7 extraction 316760 -> 242352
HEX 8 extraction 316760 -> 262246
FP turbine extr. 633520 -> 818337
adjusting flows
adjusting extractions
HEX 1 extraction 483070 -> 578256
HEX 2 extraction 477655 -> 415658
HEX 3 extraction 300658 -> 352885
HEX 4 extraction 266553 -> 240802
HEX 5 extraction 221737 -> 293722
HEX 6 extraction 309705 -> 291079
HEX 7 extraction 242352 -> 196525
HEX 8 extraction 262246 -> 221719
FP turbine extr. 818337 -> 813066
adjusting flows
adjusting extractions
HEX 1 extraction 578256 -> 613787
HEX 2 extraction 415658 -> 397713
HEX 3 extraction 352885 -> 379764
HEX 4 extraction 240802 -> 226074
HEX 5 extraction 293722 -> 311566
HEX 6 extraction 291079 -> 276074
HEX 7 extraction 196525 -> 170546
HEX 8 extraction 221719 -> 199814
FP turbine extr. 813066 -> 807258
adjusting flows
HP turbine output ......  283,718 kW
IP turbine output ......  189,376 kW
```

```
LP turbine output ......    447,609 kW
BF turbine output ......     28,585 kW
generator 1 type: 3 (    3600-rpm
conductor-cooled) rating:    475,000 KVA
shaft power input ......    473,094 kW
mechanical losses ......      1,560 kW
generator losses .......      5,876 kW
electric power output ..    465,659 kW
generator 2 type: 4 (    1800-rpm
conductor-cooled) rating:    475,000 KVA
shaft power input ......    447,609 kW
mechanical losses ......      1,560 kW
generator losses .......      4,980 kW
electric power output ..    441,069 kW
service load ..........     22,668 kW
gross power output .....    906,728 kW
net power output .......    884,060 kW
net heat input ......... 1,972,977 kW
gross heat input ....... 2,180,085 kW
turbine heatrate ....    7424.6 BTU/kWh
unit heatrate .......    8414.3 BTU/kWh
```

Several plots are automatically generated, including: inlet pressure, inlet temperature, reheat temperature, reheater pressure drop, and backpressure corrections for load and heat rate. Typical tabular and graphical results are:

Backpressure Correction to Heat Rate

TFR	backpressure	correction
-	in.HgA	%
1.00	0.5	0.3%
1.00	1.0	0.0%
1.00	1.5	1.1%
1.00	2.0	2.8%
1.00	2.5	4.6%
1.00	3.0	6.5%
1.00	3.5	8.3%
1.00	4.0	10.0%
1.00	4.5	11.7%
1.00	5.0	13.3%
0.75	0.5	-0.4%
0.75	1.0	0.0%
0.75	1.5	2.1%
0.75	2.0	4.5%
0.75	2.5	6.8%
0.75	3.0	9.1%
0.75	3.5	11.3%
0.75	4.0	13.2%

0.75	4.5	15.2%
0.75	5.0	17.1%
0.50	0.5	-2.5%
0.50	1.0	0.0%
0.50	1.5	3.5%
0.50	2.0	6.7%
0.50	2.5	9.8%
0.50	3.0	12.6%
0.50	3.5	15.3%
0.50	4.0	17.9%
0.50	4.5	20.0%
0.50	5.0	21.6%
0.25	0.5	-6.4%
0.25	1.0	0.0%
0.25	1.5	5.6%
0.25	2.0	10.8%
0.25	2.5	14.4%
0.25	3.0	17.2%
0.25	3.5	19.8%
0.25	4.0	22.1%
0.25	4.5	24.3%
0.25	5.0	26.3%

The backpressure correction to heat rate is shown in the following figure:

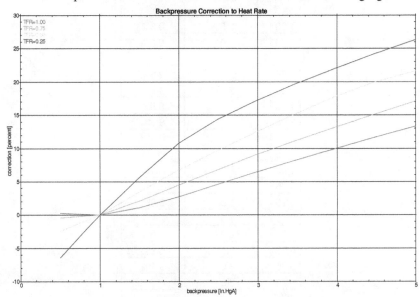

The backpressure correction to load is shown in this next figure:

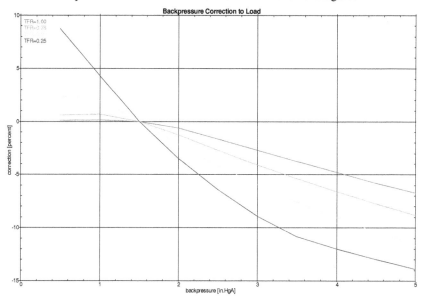

The main steam pressure correction to load is:

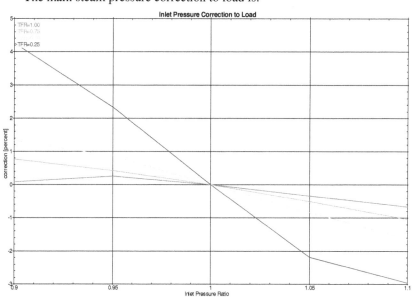

The reheat steam temperature correction to heat rate is:

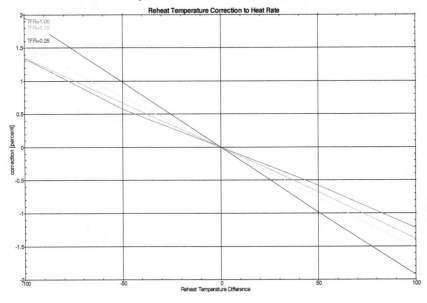

Appendix D. GT Exhaust Gas Properties

While some engineers insist on following ASME PTC-22 (2005), the properties contained therein reportedly come from the NASA Glenn report.[19] This is true, except for conversion factors and algebraic manipulation, but why not just use the original reference as is? I have provided an Excel® Add-In for all of the NASA Glenn properties. You can download it from this link:

https://dudleybenton.altervista.org/software/NASAGlenn100.zip

Note that specific heat is mass-weighted, not mole-weighted, and GT exhaust composition is most often specified in mole fractions. Mass weighting is implemented in the spreadsheet HRSG1.xls. You will also find a spreadsheet (specific_heats.xls) in the examples\gases folder. In programs HRSG3.c, HRSG4.c, and CCPP2.c we have the following code to facilitate the mole and mass fractions as well as the specific heat, enthalpy, and implicit temperature calculations.

```
typedef struct{double a,b,c,d,MW;}GAS;
GAS N2 ={-1.823844E-01,2.450080E-01,
9.515373E-06,1.278920E-09,28.013};
GAS O2 ={-1.173314E-02,2.177264E-01,
1.570874E-06,1.001867E-09,31.998};
GAS CO2={ 1.374508E-03,1.873375E-01,
3.953234E-06,1.303025E-10,44.010};
GAS H2O={ 9.393189E-05,4.431567E-01,
6.169783E-08,9.216964E-12,18.015};
GAS Ar ={ 7.922561E-14,1.242788E-01,
-2.526427E-18,9.458965E-22,39.948};
GAS SO2={ 1.495539E-05,1.417236E-01,
1.931810E-08,1.479716E-12,64.066};

double Hgas(MF mf,double T)
{
double HN2,HO2,HCO2,HH2O,HAr,HSO2,X,Y;
HN2 =(( N2.d*T+ N2.c)*T+ N2.b)*T+ N2.a;
HO2 =(( O2.d*T+ O2.c)*T+ O2.b)*T+ O2.a;
HCO2=((CO2.d*T+CO2.c)*T+CO2.b)*T+CO2.a;
HH2O=((H2O.d*T+H2O.c)*T+H2O.b)*T+H2O.a;
HAr =(( Ar.d*T+ Ar.c)*T+ Ar.b)*T+ Ar.a;
HSO2=((SO2.d*T+SO2.c)*T+SO2.b)*T+SO2.a;
X= HN2* N2.MW*mf.N2
+ HO2* O2.MW*mf.O2
+HCO2*CO2.MW*mf.CO2
+HH2O*H2O.MW*mf.H2O
+ HAr* Ar.MW*mf.Ar
+HSO2*SO2.MW*mf.SO2;
```

---

[19] McBride, B. J., Zehe, M. J., Gordon, S., "NASA Glenn Coefficients for Calculating Thermodynamic Properties of Individual Species," NASA Report No. 211556, 2002.

```
Y= N2.MW*mf.N2
 + O2.MW*mf.O2
 +CO2.MW*mf.CO2
 +H2O.MW*mf.H2O
 + Ar.MW*mf.Ar
 +SO2.MW*mf.SO2;
 return(X/Y);
 }
double Tgas(MF mf,double H)
 {
 int iter;
 double T,T1,T2;
 T1=0.;
 T2=2000.;
 for(iter=0;iter<32;iter++)
   {
   T=(T1+T2)/2.;
   if(Hgas(mf,T)<H)
     T1=T;
   else
     T2=T;
   }
 return(T);
 }
```

Combustion Chemistry

Complete combustion of hydrocarbon fuels with moist air having excess oxygen is typical of gas turbines. The chemical reactions are often generalized in terms of the average fuel composition and the H/C molar ratio (m/n in this case). This reaction can be written:

$$0.7808N_2 + 0.2095O_2 + 0.0004CO_2 + 0.0093Ar + wH_2O$$
$$+ a(Cn + Hm) = \alpha N_2 + \beta O_2 + \gamma CO_2 + \delta Ar + \varepsilon H_2O \tag{D.1}$$

$$\alpha = 0.7808$$
$$\delta = 0.0093 \tag{D.2}$$

$$\beta = 0.2095 - a\left(n + \frac{m}{2}\right)$$
$$\gamma = 0.0004 + an \tag{D.3}$$
$$\varepsilon = w + \frac{m}{2}$$

The mole fractions of the constituents can be calculated directly from these parameters. The calculations are implemented in CCPP4.c. The humidity ratio

108

must be modified to account for the differing molecular weights of dry air and water vapor. The ambient and combustion functions are listed below:

```
typedef struct{double N2,O2,CO2,H2O,Ar;}MF;

MF Ambient(double baro,double Tdb,double RH)
    {
    double W,x,y;
    static MF mf;
    W=fWdbrh(baro,Tdb,RH);
    x=W/(1.+W);
    y=x*28.9645/18.01534;
    mf.H2O=y;
    mf.N2 =0.7808*(1.-y);
    mf.O2 =0.2095*(1.-y);
    mf.CO2=0.0004*(1.-y);
    mf.Ar =0.0093*(1.-y);
    return(mf);
    }

MF Combustion(MF mf1,double Fair,double Ffuel,double
    HCratio)
    {
    double C,H,S;
    static MF mf2;
    H=HCratio/(1.+HCratio);
    C=1.-H;
    mf2.N2 =Fair*mf1.N2;
    mf2.O2 =Fair*mf1.O2 -Ffuel*(C+H/2.);
    mf2.CO2=Fair*mf1.CO2+Ffuel*C;
    mf2.Ar =Fair*mf1.Ar;
    mf2.H2O=Fair*mf1.H2O+Ffuel*H/2.;
    S=mf2.N2+mf2.O2+mf2.CO2+mf2.Ar+mf2.H2O;
    mf2.N2 /=S;
    mf2.O2 /=S;
    mf2.CO2/=S;
    mf2.Ar /=S;
    mf2.H2O/=S;
    return(mf2);
    }
```

also by D. James Benton

3D Articulation: Using OpenGL, ISBN-9798596362480, Amazon, 2021 (book 3 in the 3D series).

3D Models in Motion Using OpenGL, ISBN-9798652987701, Amazon, 2020 (book 2 in the 3D series.

3D Rendering in Windows: How to display three-dimensional objects in Windows with and without OpenGL, ISBN-9781520339610, Amazon, 2016 (book 1 in the 3D series).

A Synergy of Short Stories: The whole may be greater than the sum of the parts, ISBN-9781520340319, Amazon, 2016.

Azeotropes: Behavior and Application, ISBN-9798609748997, Amazon, 2020.

bat-Elohim: Book 3 in the Little Star Trilogy, ISBN-9781686148682, Amazon, 2019.

Boilers: Performance and Testing, ISBN: 9798789062517, Amazon 2021.

Combined 3D Rendering Series: 3D Rendering in Windows®, 3D Models in Motion, and 3D Articulation, ISBN-9798484417032, Amazon, 2021.

Complex Variables: Practical Applications, ISBN-9781794250437, Amazon, 2019.

Compression & Encryption: Algorithms & Software, ISBN-9781081008826, Amazon, 2019.

Computational Fluid Dynamics: an Overview of Methods, ISBN-9781672393775, Amazon, 2019.

Computer Simulation of Power Systems: Programming Strategies and Practical Examples, ISBN-9781696218184, Amazon, 2019.

Contaminant Transport: A Numerical Approach, ISBN-9798461733216, Amazon, 2021.

CPUnleashed! Tapping Processor Speed, ISBN-9798421420361, Amazon, 2022.

Curve-Fitting: The Science and Art of Approximation, ISBN-9781520339542, Amazon, 2016.

Death by Tie: It was the best of ties. It was the worst of ties. It's what got him killed., ISBN-9798398745931, Amazon, 2023.

Differential Equations: Numerical Methods for Solving, ISBN-9781983004162, Amazon, 2018.

Equations of State: A Graphical Comparison, ISBN-9798843139520, Amazon, 2022.

Evaporative Cooling: The Science of Beating the Heat, ISBN-9781520913346, Amazon, 2017.

Forecasting: Extrapolation and Projection, ISBN-9798394019494, Amazon 2023.

Heat Engines: Thermodynamics, Cycles, & Performance Curves, ISBN-9798486886836, Amazon, 2021.

Heat Exchangers: Performance Prediction & Evaluation, ISBN-9781973589327, Amazon, 2017.

Heat Recovery Steam Generators: Thermal Design and Testing, ISBN-9781691029365, Amazon, 2019.

Heat Transfer: Heat Exchangers, Heat Recovery Steam Generators, & Cooling Towers, ISBN-9798487417831, Amazon, 2021.

Heat Transfer Examples: Practical Problems Solved, ISBN-9798390610763, Amazon, 2023.

The Kick-Start Murders: Visualize revenge, ISBN-9798759083375, Amazon, 2021.

Jamie2: Innocence is easily lost and cannot be restored, ISBN-9781520339375, Amazon, 2016-18.

Kyle Cooper Mysteries: Kick Start, Monte Carlo, and Waterfront Murders, ISBN-9798829365943, Amazon, 2022.

The Last Seraph: Sequel to Little Star, ISBN-9781726802253, Amazon, 2018.

Little Star: God doesn't do things the way we expect Him to. He's better than that! ISBN-9781520338903, Amazon, 2015-17.

Living Math: Seeing mathematics in every day life (and appreciating it more too), ISBN-9781520336992, Amazon, 2016.

Lost Cause: If only history could be changed..., ISBN-9781521173770, Amazon, 2017.

Mass Transfer: Diffusion & Convection, ISBN-9798702403106, Amazon, 2021.

Mill Town Destiny: The Hand of Providence brought them together to rescue the mill, the town, and each other, ISBN-9781520864679, Amazon, 2017.

Monte Carlo Murders: Who Killed Who and Why, ISBN-9798829341848, Amazon, 2022.

Monte Carlo Simulation: The Art of Random Process Characterization, ISBN-9781980577874, Amazon, 2018.

Nonlinear Equations: Numerical Methods for Solving, ISBN-9781717767318, Amazon, 2018.

Numerical Calculus: Differentiation and Integration, ISBN-9781980680901, Amazon, 2018.

Numerical Methods: Nonlinear Equations, Numerical Calculus, & Differential Equations, ISBN-9798486246845, Amazon, 2021.

Orthogonal Functions: The Many Uses of, ISBN-9781719876162, Amazon, 2018.

Overwhelming Evidence: A Pilgrimage, ISBN-9798515642211, Amazon, 2021.

Particle Tracking: Computational Strategies and Diverse Examples, ISBN-9781692512651, Amazon, 2019.

Plumes: Delineation & Transport, ISBN-9781702292771, Amazon, 2019.

Power Plant Performance Curves: for Testing and Dispatch, ISBN-9798640192698, Amazon, 2020.

Practical Linear Algebra: Principles & Software, ISBN-9798860910584, Amazon, 2023.

Props, Fans, & Pumps: Design & Performance, ISBN-9798645391195, Amazon, 2020.

Remediation: Contaminant Transport, Particle Tracking, & Plumes, ISBN-9798485651190, Amazon, 2021.

ROFL: Rolling on the Floor Laughing, ISBN-9781973300007, Amazon, 2017.

Seminole Rain: You don't choose destiny. It chooses you, ISBN-9798668502196, Amazon, 2020.

Septillionth: 1 in 10^{24}, ISBN-9798410762472, Amazon, 2022.

Software Development: Targeted Applications, ISBN-9798850653989, Amazon, 2023.

Software Recipes: Proven Tools, ISBN-9798815229556, Amazon, 2022.

Steam 2020: to 150 GPa and 6000 K, ISBN-9798634643830, Amazon, 2020.

Thermochemical Reactions: Numerical Solutions, ISBN-9781073417872, Amazon, 2019.

Thermodynamic and Transport Properties of Fluids, ISBN-9781092120845, Amazon, 2019.

Thermodynamic Cycles: Effective Modeling Strategies for Software Development, ISBN-9781070934372, Amazon, 2019.

Thermodynamics - Theory & Practice: The science of energy and power, ISBN-9781520339795, Amazon, 2016.

Version-Independent Programming: Code Development Guidelines for the Windows® Operating System, ISBN-9781520339146, Amazon, 2016.

The Waterfront Murders: As you sow, so shall you reap, ISBN-9798611314500, Amazon, 2020.

Weather Data: Where To Get It and How To Process It, ISBN-9798868037894, Amazon, 2023.